JN329845

手を加えた自然にこそ自然がある
UEJI, The Genius of Water and Stone

シリーズ・京の庭の巨匠たち 2
The Great Masters of Gardens of Kyoto 2

植治
七代目 小川治兵衞

京都通信社
K.T.P. Books
Kyoto Tsushinsha Press

植治 七代目小川治兵衞
(1860-1933)

明治も間近い1860年、京都近郊の長岡京市に山本源之助として生まれる。咸臨丸が日米条約批准のために勝麟太郎らを乗せて太平洋に乗り出した年である。やがて、17歳で養子として入った小川家は江戸中期からつづく植木屋、屋号は「植治」。しかし、ほどなく養父は急逝。19歳で七代目小川治兵衞を襲名するも、師はいない。独学で作庭法を学ぶうちに、長州の政商・久原庄三郎を介して、欧米の事情や文化を視野に入れつつ行動する山縣有朋、中井弘、伊集院兼常ら薩長出身の政財界人と出会い、新しい時代の思潮、西欧的な暮らしを学び、作庭観を一変させる。同時に、山縣らがそうであったように、異文化を知ることで逆に、日本の伝統文化と美意識に自らのアイデンティティを求めた。維新という革命をへたこの時代は、新しいものを受け入れることに躊躇しない革新と変革の時代。植治は、政財界人や華族の庭のみならず、円山公園などの公共庭園を扱うことで、まったく新しい日本庭園の姿を生み出す開拓者となった。その植治の精神は、現在の十一代目小川治兵衞氏と小川勝章氏が受け継ぐ。

Ueji, OGAWA Jihei VII
(1860-1933)

OGAWA Jihei VII, also known as Ueji, was born in 1860, just before the Meiji Restoration. His former name was YAMAMOTO Gennosuke. He was adopted by the OGAWAs, a traditional gardening family, at the age of 17. He became head of the family at the young age of 19 after the sudden death of his father in law, OGAWA Jihei VI. He learned landscape gardening on his own but through his relatives he made the acquaintance of some of the most important businessmen and statesmen of the Meiji era. This new high society was equally knowledgeable about occidental manners and Japanese traditions. Ueji immediately understood their need for a new type of garden. He transformed the traditional Japanese garden according to the taste of his epoch, with bright, wide-open spaces incorporating lawns and water. He was the pioneer of the modern Japanese garden. Ueji's name became famous and he created both private and public gardens throughout Japan. Today, OGAWA Jihei XI and his son OGAWA Katsuaki are continuing in the spirit of his work.

植治、自らを語る

黒田天外　美術評論家

　明治四十三年四月一日夜、関西切ての園藝の名家、小川治兵衛氏を白川、畔の宅に訪ふ。床に翁[1]「無事便深山」の五字幅を掛けたるが、語意隽永にして坐ろに主人の心地を想はしむ。主人と余と十数年の夙好、昵々として語る。曰く、

　お話のやうに園藝も大分進歩して参りました。昔、小堀遠州が桂の離宮を造るに三年かゝつたと云ひますが、なに金さへあつたらそんなにかゝらずとも今日ではもつと早く出来ます、先づざつと地面を見渡した處で、此庭園はどう作るがよい、こゝの處は何の石がよい、こゝの處は何の樹がよい、こゝをかう疎にして、こゝをかう密にして、こゝに流れをつけて、こゝに池を作つて、月は何處から上る、秋になるとどの邊になる、日光でも日の長い時はどう、短い時はどう、そして費用はどうと、長年やつて居ることでございますから、大概目算がつきまさァ。それに庭園に定つた好みなどないのは、一に地形によるからでございます。

　今度住友さんが茶臼山に別荘[2]をこしらへられるのでございますが、総地坪が四万坪で、其の半分の二万坪は庭園になるのでございますから、昔なら秀吉公の仕事どすな。私のいつたのは昨年からですが、全部任すといふことで先づ三年位はかゝります。何分大阪城を築いた地勢ほどあつて、庭石でも四国からどんどん五千貫、七千貫といふのが何百と知れん程集まつてまさァ、あれが出来れば関西第一で、岡山公園など兎ても及びますまい。

　ヘィ、私は乙訓郡西神足村[3]、字馬場山本彌兵衞の三男[4]で、幼名源之助と云ひました。槇村知事[5]の時分に、私と他の者二人とを郡から選抜して、何か学問をやらすとのことでしたが、私は学問よりかう云ふ方が好でそれを断はり、十七の歳に小川家へ入家[6]して、先代の名の治兵衞に改めました。この小川家は私で五代目[7]になりますので、初めは園藝の稽古も、やはり天

黒田天外（くろだ・てんがい）、本名・譲　美術評論家であり小説家、宗教家。本文は、天外著『續々江湖快心録』（1922年）所載の「園藝の名家」から抜粋した。読み仮名は編集部の判断による。漢字は新字に置き換えたが、ほかは原文のまま。『江湖快心録』は、本編のほか、續、續々の三部作。明治期の京都の画家、工芸家などの聞き書きを数多く残した。

KURODA Tengai was an art critic, novelist, and person of religion. KURODA wrote down many talks by Kyoto-based artists of the Meiji era.

Words of Ueji

KURODA Tengai
Art critic

　On the evening of April 1, 1910, I visited OGAWA Jihei, or Ueji, the most prominent landscape artist in the Kansai region, at his house by the Shirakawa River. This is what he said.

　The art of landscaping has, as you say, made much progress. They say that it took three years for KOBORI Enshū[1] to build the Katsura Imperial Villa. If budget were not an issue, today we could construct it much faster than that. First, I pass my eye over the land. I have years of experience so it takes only a minute to form a general plan for how to create a garden on the site; what stones to place, what trees to plant, where to group things, where to spread them out, where to cut a stream, and where to dig a pond. Then I check where the moon rises, where it is in the fall, where the sun shines in warm seasons and in cold seasons. Finally, I estimate how much it will cost. By the way, each garden has its own ambience, so I stick to no definite form, because it depends on the geographic features of the land.

　Mr. SUMITOMO is planning to build a villa in Osaka. A 130,000 m^2 villa, half of it will be a garden. It is a project comparable to those undertaken by some powerful feudal lords. I met Mr. SUMITOMO last year. He said he would leave it entirely up to me. I think it will take three years or so. The site is the same size as the grounds of Osaka Castle. Hundreds of garden stones weighing around 2 to 3 tons are being sent from Shikoku. When completed, the garden will be the greatest in the Kansai region. Even the renowned Kōraku-en garden in Okayama will not compare to it at all.

　I was born in Nagaoka-kyō in the suburbs of Kyoto as the second son of YAMAMOTO Tōgorō. My childhood name was Gennosuke. When MAKIMURA Masanao was the governor of Kyoto Prefecture, the country gave two other boys and I

何有荘の蹲踞

A crouching basin
covered with moss in Kaiu-sō

the chance to do some academic studies. I declined the offer because I preferred jobs like this to studying. When I was seventeen, I married into the OGAWA family and changed my name to Jihei, the same as the previous head of the family. I became the seventh head of the OGAWA family. At first, I learned the basics of traditional landscaping, such as *tenchijin*[2] and *gogyō*[3] as practice for gardening. Until my mid-thirties it was common for me to climb trees with scissors in my hands. But a change occurred when YAMAGATA Aritomo asked me to plant 50 five-foot fir-trees in Murin-an, the garden he had planned. At that time, since it was uncommon to use firs as garden trees, they were not readily available. I made a great effort to gather fir-trees from various quarters. Nowadays, they are frequently seen even in ordinary gardens. Azaleas, hollies, and nandinas are also used. In fact, YAMAGATA pioneered their use as garden trees.

Later, when the Heian-jingū Shrine built its garden, they decided to call the plantsman taking care of YAMAGATA's villa garden, which happened to be me. The more than 10,000 m² site couldn't be completed for around one thousand yen. I asked them to double the budget; they said "No." It was painful, but I managed to finish the job. Then I was asked to build a garden for the museum. I somehow worked it out on a rough 33,000 m² field in one or one and a half months. It was around that time that I began to enjoy fame.

The museum garden was followed successively by KUHARA's, SHIMIZU's and ICHIDA's gardens. In addition, I rehabilitated TANAKA's garden. They are successful Kyoto and Osaka-based businessmen. Today I am constantly engaged in building one or two gardens, and send my staff to Momoyama, Osaka, Suma, Tarumi, and Mikage, as well as Kyoto. In late March, I designed the garden of a VIP room for the Toyama municipal government. For what I am now, I am grateful to three people. They are YAMAGATA Aritomo, NAKAI Hiroshi, and IJŪIN Kanetsune. IJŪIN is a master, a rare master. His constructions and his

地人*とか、五行*とかいふことを正直に学んでやつて居り、また三十四五まではやはり樹へ昇つてチョキンチョキンとやつて居りました。處が山縣[8]さんが無隣庵をお作りになることゝなり、五尺くらゐの樅を五十本栽へろといふ仰せつけでしたが、其頃樅などゝいふものは庭木につかいませんので一向なく、漸やく方々から集めて調へましたが、只今では何處の庭園でも樅を多く用ひ、またどうだん、柊、南天などを使ひますのも、山縣さんが嚆矢でございます。

その後平安神宮の神園を作るにつき、山縣さんへ行て居る植木屋を呼べとのことで私が命ぜられましたが、三千坪からの處を千圓や千五百圓[9]でいけさうな筈がない、丁度倍額ほど入たが出してくれといふても出してくれませず、其頃は未だ隨分苦痛でございましたが忍んで之をやり上げますと、今度は博物館[10]の庭園を作れとのことで一万坪からあつて野原のやうな處を一月や一月半でやつてのけましたが、此頃から少し私の名が知れましてございます。

つゞいて、久原[11]さんの庭、清水[12]さんの庭、市田[13]さんの庭と追々作り、田中[14]さんの庭もなほす、其他今日で

4

は京都は固より、桃山、大阪、須磨、垂水、御影と各處に人をやつて、大抵一軒や二軒の庭を造つて居り、この三月の末には富山縣庁の貴賓室の庭園も設計致しました。それで私が今日にまでなりましたのは、全く山縣さん、中井弘(15)さん、伊集院兼常(16)さん、此の御三人の御蔭で、伊集院さん程の名人は滅多にございません。普請といひ、庭園といひ、先づ近世の遠州公どすな。

昔の庭園など寂がつくので自然によい筈で、假令ば木一本でも、風に揉まれ、雨に打れ、根は張る、枝は茂る、自づとよくなります、其事を思ふと、今やつたやつはよいとせんなりまへん。夫に庭園などでも時勢につれて變更せんならんので、今日では寂一方ではいきまへん、やつぱり園遊会でお客の二三百人ぐらゐいれる芝原の必要も生じて来ますから、此方では市田さんの庭など少しも差支へありませぬ。

私は阿誰にも遠慮せん方で、氣張てまともの事をしたら、三つの御辭儀を四つせんならんことはない。而して大きな處に目度をつけて、心で小さく踏でいきます。何分此家を先祖から受取たのやから、夫を辱かしめん様にやりたいつもりで、平日でも代物(17)しこむにも骨が折れゝば、新奇な燈籠にもいろいろ考案を運らさねばならず、両方やつて居るからどつちも十分にいけんのどす、然し年は未だ五十一ですから、まだまだ之からやりますつもりで。

ハイ、俺の白楊も病身であつたから写真をやらせましたが、お陰で身体は壮健になり、また写真をとるに位置を苦心しましたのが、計らず庭園を作る上について大きに役に立て、考へが早くつきます、それで私の代理に方々へやつて居りますので、と。

氏質性撲実堅確にして、毫も賈飾を用ひざるも、実力名技の在る處、富豪貴紳争ふて礼を厚くし之を聘し、其作意に成る名園今日既に十餘を以て数へ、小なるものは僂指するに暇あらず、実に造園の名家と言ふべし。談話三時許、辞し帰る。

1) 菘翁　貫名菘翁(1778-1863年)のこと。江戸時代の書家で幕末の三筆の一人。
2) 別荘　住友家第15代当主の住友春翠別邸「慶沢園」庭園のこと。1909-1910年に作庭。規模は小さくなったが、天王寺公園の一部として公開されている。
3) 乙訓郡西神足村　現在の長岡京市。
4) 山本彌右衛門の三男　正しくは山本藤五郎の二男。
5) 槇村知事　京都府の第二代知事を務めた槇村正直(1834-1896)のこと。長州の人。
6) 入家　婿入りすること。
7) 小川家五代目　正しくは七代目。
8) 山縣　38ページ参照。
9) 千五百圓　10ページ参照。小野氏が10ページに掲載している資料によると、植治は最終的に1,703円56銭の見積書を提出したようだ。
10) 博物館　現在の京都国立博物館のこと。1896年着手。
11) 久原　明治の実業家、久原庄三郎(1840-1908年)のこと。若き植治を山縣有朋の庭を作庭することになった。長州の人。
12) 清水　明治・大正期の大阪の実業家、清水吉次郎(1875-1949年)のこと。植治に「十牛庵」(現・高台寺土井)の作庭を依頼。
13) 市田　実業家の市田弥一郎(1843-1906年)のこと。植治に對龍山荘の作庭を依頼した。
14) 田中　大阪の実業家であり政治家田中市兵衞(1838-1909年)のこと。角倉了以のかつての本邸を購入し植治に作庭を依頼した。
15) 中井弘　京都府の第五代知事を務めた中井弘(1840-1894年)のこと。薩摩の人。
16) 伊集院兼常　薩摩出身の明治の政商。植治に作庭の知識と考え方、機会を与えた。1836-1909年。
17) 代物　材料、販売する商品のこと。

gardening style prove he is the KOBORI Enshū of the modern age.

Ancient gardens that mellow with age are naturally good. For instance, trees blown by winds and exposed to rain for years root firmly and have thick branches. They are naturally good. Taking this into consideration, new gardens are good as they are, but only reach perfection with age. In addition, landscaping must change with the times. Today *wabi sabi*[4] is not necessarily almighty. When a garden party is held for two to three hundred guests, the need arises for a lawn area. In this sense, ICHIDA's garden is perfect.

I am not too polite to anyone. After doing one's best, one doesn't need to bow four times when three are enough. I tell myself to see the big picture and to proceed gradually with heart. This establishment was passed down to me from the ancestors. I try not to disgrace its name. On workdays, I am busy keeping goods in stock on the one hand, and racking my brain for new ideas, say for new styles of garden lantern, on the other. As I do both, neither of them is very good. But I am only fifty-one, so I still have a long way to go.

My son Hakuyō had a weak constitution, so I allowed him to become a photographer. Later he became healthy. The struggle to find good compositions unintentionally turned out to be very helpful in producing ideas for landscaping. Accordingly, I send him everywhere as my proxy.

He is simple, has an unbending stance, and uses no flattery. Nevertheless, the rich and noble receive with the utmost courtesy this man of proficiency and masterly skill. He has completed more than a dozen notable gardens and countless small ones. He is truly a master landscape artist.

Notes
1. KOBORI Enshū Masakazu (1579-1647) was a feudal lord and a notable artist of the beginning of the Edo period. He excelled in the arts of tea ceremony, painting, poetry, flower arrangement, and garden design.
2. *Tenchijin*: a landscaping principle of depicting the universe by incorporating elements representing the heaven, earth and humankind.
3. *Gogyō*: a philosophy explaining all events as interactions of five elements: wood, fire, earth, metal, and water. A basic landscaping principle.
4. *Wabi sabi*: a Japanese aesthetic concept in which beauty is acquired as a patina over time.

もくじ

◆植治、自らを語る 3
黒田天外　美術評論家

◆七代目小川治兵衞 7
小野健吉　文化庁文化財部記念物課主任文化財調査官

◆五感で味わう庭——植治の感性表現と意匠 13
尼﨑博正　京都造形芸術大学日本庭園・歴史遺産研究センター所長

◆庭と解説
並河靖之七宝記念館庭園 18
無鄰庵庭園 30
平安神宮神苑 42
何有荘庭園（旧和楽庵） 52
円山公園 64
碧雲荘庭園（野村別邸） 72
高台寺土井庭園（旧十牛庵） 80
「葵殿庭園」と「佳水園庭園」（ウェスティン都ホテル京都） 88

◆文化的景観としての植治の「自然」〈座談会〉 96
白幡洋三郎　国際日本文化研究センター教授
笹岡隆甫　華道未生流笹岡家元嗣
谷　晃　野村美術館学芸部長、茶の湯文化学会会長
永田　萠　イラストレーター、絵本作家

◆植治の生涯と仕事 111

◆時代思潮と植治 114
白幡洋三郎

◆庭園用語の解説 116

◆掲載庭園の所在地と交通案内 118

◆インタビュー
並河靖之氏を屋敷に訪ぬ　黒田天外 26
「変化」を許容する表現素材　永田　萠 41
植治の庭はビオトープ　森本幸裕 49
きき上手な植治はん　佐野藤右衛門 67
得庵の夢を庭に開花させた植治　谷　晃 79
「用」を備えた枯流れは、植治の真骨頂でしょう　矢ヶ崎善太郎 84
いけばなに通じる植治と白楊の自然観　笹岡隆甫 94

CONTENTS

◆Words of Ueji 3
KURODA Tengai (Art critic)

◆OGAWA Jihei VII 7
ONO Kenkichi (Senior Cultural Properties Specialist, Monuments and Sites Division, Cultural Properties Department, Agency for Cultural Affairs)

◆Garden's for All Five Senses—Ueji's Design Insights 13
AMASAKI Hiromasa (Director of the Research Center for Japanese Garden Art and Historical Heritage, Kyoto University of Art and Design)

◆Gardens
Namikawa Cloisonné Museum of Kyoto Garden 18
Murin-an Garden 30
Heian-jingū Garden 42
Kaiu-sō Garden 52
Maruyama Park 64
Hekiun-sō Garden 72
Kōdaiji-Doi Garden 80
Westin Miyako Kyoto Gardens 88

◆Creating Nature: Ueji and Kyoto Culture (Discussion) 96
SHIRAHATA Yōzaburō (Professor, International Center for Japanese Researches)
TANI Akira (Curator, Nomura Art Museum)
NAGATA Moe (Illustrator)
SASAOKA Ryūho (Master of ikebana, Japanese flower arrangement)

◆Ueji's time line (Japanese only) 111

◆The Spirit of the Meiji Era and Ueji 114
SHIRAHATA Yōzaburō (Professor, International Research Center for Japanese Studies)

◆Glossary of technical terms for Japanese gardens (Japanese only) 116

◆Locations and Access 118

Japanese names appear in their conventional order, that is, family name first.
To make a clear distinction, family names are written in small capitals.

文中に掲載の諸氏の敬称は省略しました。
本文中で＊がついている用語の説明は、
巻末の「庭園用語の解説」に掲載しています。

七代目小川治兵衞

小野健吉　文化庁文化財部記念物課主任文化財調査官

　1860年（万延元年）4月5日、のちの「植治」こと七代目小川治兵衞は、山城国西神足村（現・京都府長岡京市）で山本藤五郎の次男として生を受ける。幼名源之助。万延元年といえば、ペリーの来航から7年。幕府軍艦咸臨丸を伴走させたアメリカの軍艦に搭乗した使節が渡米し、日米修交通商条約を批准した年である。まさに幕末、動乱の時節であった。
　1877年（明治10）、源之助は三条白川橋の造園業・小川家の婿養子に入り、翌々年に家督を相続、小川治兵衞を襲名する。ちなみに、東京遷都後なんとか京都の衰退に歯止めをかけようと様々な近代化策の先頭に立つ槇村正直が京都府知事に任命されたのも1877年であった。1880年に槇村の後任として知事となった北垣国道も、槇村の殖産興業策を引き継いで京都の近代化に尽力する。なかでも、琵琶湖と京都を水路で結ぶ琵琶湖疏水を計画し、田辺朔郎[1]を起用して1885年に起工、1890年に第一期工事を竣工させたことは特筆すべき北垣の事績であり、このことが植治の活躍の重要な基盤となる。

疏水を引いた並河邸と無鄰庵の庭園

　植治がこの疏水の水を初めて庭園に活用したのは、1894年（明治27）に竣工した植治の隣家の並河靖之邸でのこと。青蓮院宮[2]の近侍をつとめていた並河は明治維新後は七宝工芸作家に転身し、この

並河邸の庭は植治が山縣に出会う前の初期の作品
Namikawa's garden is one of the first creations by Ueji

小野健吉（おの・けんきち）1955年、和歌山県に生まれる。京都大学農学部林学科卒業、奈良文化財研究所保存修復工学研究室長などをへて現職。農学博士。専門は日本庭園史。主な著書に『岩波日本庭園辞典』、『植治の庭、小川治兵衞の世界』（共著）、『醍醐寺大観』（共著）、『古都発掘』（共著）、『古代庭園の思想』（共著）、『環境デザイン学』（共著）などがある。

Ono Kenkichi : Born in 1955 in Wakayama Prefecture. Doctor of Agriculture, graduated from the Department of Forestry, Faculty of Agriculture, Kyoto University. Specialist in Japanese garden history.

OGAWA Jihei VII

ONO Kenkichi
Senior Cultural Properties Specialist, Monuments and Sites Division, Cultural Properties Department, Agency for Cultural Affairs.

　OGAWA Jihei VII, or Ueji, was born on April 5, 1860 in Nagaoka-kyō City, Kyoto Prefecture as the second son of YAMAMOTO Tōgorō. His childhood name was Gennosuke. Japan was in the last, turbulent days of the Tokugawa shogunate.
　In 1877, Gennosuke married into the OGAWA landscaping family, based in Kyoto. In 1879 he inherited the family estate, succeeding to the OGAWA Jihei name. After the capital was relocated to Tokyo, Kyoto governors took the lead on modernization measures to prevent Kyoto's decline. The most noteworthy project was the excavation of a canal between Lake Biwa and Kyoto. Construction commenced in 1885 and the first stage of the project was completed in 1890. The Lake Biwa Canal later served as an important foundation for Ueji's great success.

Water Used in Gardens at the NAMIKAWA House and Murin-an Villa
　Ueji used water from the Lake Biwa Canal as a landscaping component for the first time at NAMIKAWA Yasuyuki's house, completed in 1894. NAMIKAWA was valet to an Imperial prince until the Meiji Restoration, after which he became a cloisonné artist. Around the time he built his house, he was the greatest cloisonné artist of the period, receiving numerous awards in Japan and abroad. Since NAMIKAWA's house was also his cloisonné studio, water was diverted from the canal for use in polishing. Ueji redirected the water to build a garden pond.
　The two-story main building of the NAMIKAWA house is built over the pond to the southwest, creating a sense of integration between building and garden. To the east, the house commands a view of the Higashiyama hills through the trees. Notable design features are: a large island relative to the size of the pond, stones surfacing through the water, and a pointed blue-

ころには国内外で数々の賞を受けた当代きっての実力者となっていた。並河邸は七宝工房も兼ねていたため、工房で研磨用水として導入していた疏水の水を、植治は庭の池水として利用したのである。

並河邸は、二階建ての主屋をその南西側の池に乗り出すように配置し、建築と庭園とが一体化した空間を形成、東方には木立越しに東山を望むことができる。デザイン的には、池の面積に比べて大ぶりな中島や池に浮かぶ岩島、南岸の山天[3]の青石の立石が目を引く。疏水の水を導入したとはいえ、こうした構成はどちらかといえば京都の近世の寺院庭園などに近いかもしれない。いずれにせよ、植治は施主の求めに応じて、伝統的な京都の庭園を築造する十分な技量をもっていたことが、この庭園から見て取れる。

技量豊かな庭師として法然院や実業家久原庄三郎邸などに出入りしていた植治は、1894年、その久原の紹介で明治の元勲山縣有朋の京都別邸「無鄰庵」の造園にたずさわることになる。久原は長州藩出身で、山縣とは同郷であった。ところが、その年7月に日清戦争が勃発、山縣は京都に来られる状況ではなくなり、山縣から造園の指示を託された久原庄三郎が植治を使って工事に着手することになる。

1895年(明治28)には建築工事も進み、8月には琵琶湖疏水から無鄰庵への導水が京都市の事業として完了、庭園は一番奥に当たる東端部を除いて一応のかたちを整える。疏水引き込みについての京都市の積極的な関与は、この地域一帯を良好な宅地としようという京都市の都市政策を反映したものであった。

庭園東端部は、1895年12月ごろから工事に着手。それから約1年、山縣の指揮監督を随時受けながら造園工事は進行し、1896年末には一応の完成を見る。そして、翌春に山縣自らが検分、手直しを加えて、最終的な完成に至ったのである。

無鄰庵庭園と植治の能力を引き出した施主たち

無鄰庵の造園について、後年山縣自身が語ったところが美術評論家・黒田天外によって記録されている。要約すると、「この庭園の主山は東山であり、山麓にあるこの庭園では、滝も水も東山から出てきたようにデザインする必要があり、石の配置、樹木の配植も自ずと決まってくる」、「滝の岩の間に歯朶(シダ)を植え、躑躅(ツツジ)を岩に付着するように植える。地被としては、苔ではなく芝を用いる。樅(モミ)を用いるとともに、杉・楓(カエデ)・葉桜を植栽の中心とする」、「山村を流れる川のイメージで、池ではなく流れの庭とする」といったことがらである。

このうち第1点目は、山縣が造園の本質を深く理解していたことを示している。すなわち、造園デザインにおいては、中心となる要素が決まれば他の要素はそれにしたがって自ずと割り出される、という認識である。山縣はその認識のうえで、この庭園の中心要素を敷地の外にある東山と定め、敷地の狭小さを補い、予想外の雄大さをこの庭に与えたのである。

第2点目、第3点目は、象徴主義的手法から脱却し、写実的手法で心地よい空間を創出しようとする山縣の好尚を示している。この山縣の好尚は、ひとり山縣

green stone standing on the south bank. Although the garden makes use of canal water, the composition somewhat resembles that of pre-modern temple gardens in Kyoto. It is evident that Ueji had the skill to build traditional Kyoto-style gardens, if they were requested.

A skilled gardener, Ueji took care of the Honen-in temple garden and the house of businessman KUHARA Shōzaburō. In 1894, KUHARA introduced Ueji to YAMAGATA Aritomo, one of the greatest members of the Meiji government. In July 1894, YAMAGATA had to leave for the Japan-Chinese War, but on KUHARA's recommendation he entrusted Ueji with the construction of the garden for Murin-an, his villa in Kyoto.

In August of the following year, 1895, a ditch from the canal to Murin-an was completed as a public works project. The garden came close to its completed form. The positive involvement of the municipal government in the use of canal water for the villa was indicative of the government's urban development policy, aimed at turning the surrounding area into a prime residential district.

The construction of the garden's east end commenced around December 1895. With occasional supervision by YAMAGATA the landscaping work was mainly completed by the end of 1896 and perfected the following spring, after YAMAGATA's inspection and some alterations.

The Murin-an Garden, Ueji's Ability, and Clients Who Helped Him Achieve His Potential

The art critic KURODA Tengai recorded these comments by YAMAGATA about the landscaping at Murin-an: "The main feature of this garden is the Higashiyama hills. Flows of water, including waterfalls, must be designed as if they come from Higashiyama since this garden is at the foot of the hills. Accordingly, the layout of stones and trees is clear...Plant ferns among the stones of the waterfall and azaleas very close to the stones. Cover the ground with a lawn rather than moss. Use fir trees. It is important to plant cedar, maple, and cherry trees... The garden should incorporate flows of water, like a creek through a mountain village, rather than a pond."

The first remark reveals that YAMAGATA had a deep understanding of the essentials of landscaping. More specifically, he knew that in landscape design the first thing to do is choose the

無鄰庵の滝石組の隙間にシダを植えて山の自然の風景を演出する手法は、山縣に学んだ
Ferns were planted intentionally amongst the stones of the waterfall at Murin-an

だけのものではなく、明治時代の東京における新興有産階級の好尚であった。1910年（明治43）に刊行された『名園五十種』のなかで、著者近藤正一は明治時代に築造された東京の庭園を数多く取り上げ、写実的手法を用いた庭園を「天然趣味」、「自然趣味」の呼称でとりまとめ、高い評価を与えている。山縣が東京目白に営んだ自邸「椿山荘」はその代表格であり、山縣がこうした好尚を牽引する役割を果たしていたことも事実であろう。

京都のそれまでの伝統的な造園手法のなかで生きてきた植治にとって、山縣の主張する庭園デザインは、やはり異質なものであった。山縣の述懐として、「石組みには陰石・陽石・五石・七石など様々な法則がある」と植治が主張したことや、岩と岩の間にシダを植えたりモミを群植したりといった山縣の指示に、植治が初めは驚いたことなどが記されている。しかし、植治は山縣の好尚とそれに基づく庭園デザインを理解し、蓄えてきた庭師としての技量によってそれに応える。その背景には、植治の生来の頭の良さとともに、伊集院兼常や久原など、それまで接する機会のあった新興有産階級に属する人々からそうした好尚の一端を伝え聞いていたことがあったのかもしれない。ちなみに、伊集院兼常は、薩摩出身で、明治時代には海軍省営繕局長や日本土木会社社長を歴任。建築や庭園にすぐれ、京都では廣誠院や初期の對龍山荘

main element; it is then possible to determine the other features without difficulty. Based on this understanding, YAMAGATA had the daring to use the Higashiyama hills outside his garden as its main element, increasing the apparent land area and producing an unexpectedly spacious garden.

The second and third remarks indicate that YAMAGATA particularly enjoyed creating comfortable spaces through naturalistic techniques, rather than by symbolic means. YAMAGATA was not the only one with this idea. It was a preference of the emerging Tokyo-based propertied class of the Meiji period. A book written by KONDŌ Shōichi, published in 1910, discusses fifty notable gardens, many of which were built in Tokyo during the Meiji period. KONDŌ gave high praise to gardens constructed using naturalistic techniques. Chinzan-sō, YAMAGATA's house in Tokyo, is a representative example. YAMAGATA must have played a leading role in promoting such preferences.

For Ueji, who had been pursuing traditional landscape design in Kyoto, YAMAGATA's assertions about garden design were not readily acceptable at first. According to YAMAGATA's reflections, Ueji originally insisted that traditional rules should apply to stone arrangements, and he was astonished by YAMAGATA's instructions to plant ferns among stones and to use large numbers of fir trees. Nonetheless, Ueji understood both YAMAGATA's preferences and the resulting garden design, and responded positively to YAMAGATA's expectations with his wealth of gardening skill.

Murin-an was the result of the integration of YAMAGATA's concept and Ueji's skill at the foot of the Higashiyama hills in Kyoto, where a new environment was brought about by the completion of the Lake Biwa Canal. The Murin-an garden was an epoch-making event in the history of modern Japanese landscaping.

Ueji's Ability as Producer Proven by the Heian-jingū Shrine Gardens

When Ueji's involvement in the construction of the Murin-an garden began, preparations for the 1,100th anniversary of the establishment of Heian-kyō (the old name for Kyoto) were under way in Okazaki. One of the core projects for the anniversary was the construction of the Heian-jingū Shrine, including a commemorative hall

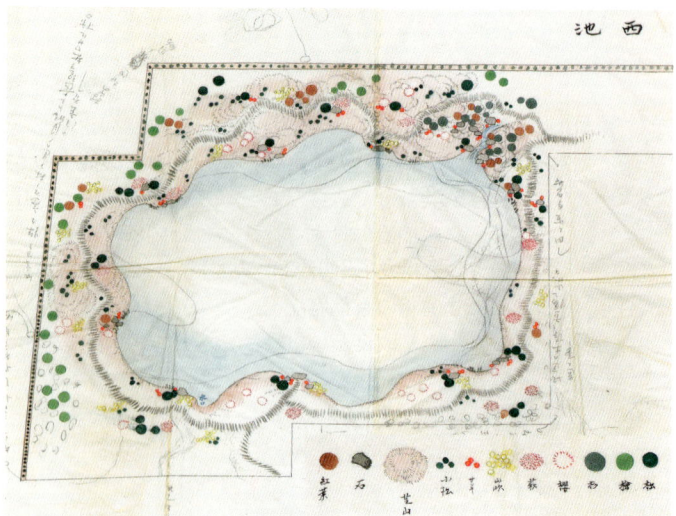

植治が平安神宮に提出した平安神宮西神苑のイメージ図(左)と植栽の配置図(右)〈資料提供・平安神宮〉
Ueji's plans for the West Garden of Heian-jingū

平安神宮東神苑では、栖鳳池とそこに架かる橋殿が平安王朝風の雰囲気を醸し出す
View of the East Garden of Heian-jingū

を造営した人物である。

ともあれ、琵琶湖疏水の完成により新たな環境を整えた京都東山山麓に、山縣の構想と植治の技量が融合して創出された無鄰庵庭園は、近代庭園のひとつの画期をなしたのである。

平安神宮神苑で見せたプロデューサー的力量

植治が無鄰庵の造園にかかわりはじめたころ、岡崎では平安奠都千年紀念祭に向けた準備が進められていた。紀念祭に合わせて企画された第四回内国勧業博覧会とともに、その中心的な事業となったのが平安宮大極殿を8分の5に縮小した紀念殿、すなわち平安神宮拝殿などの造営事業である。1893年に地鎮祭、翌年に立柱式が行われるが、建物の背後を取り巻く庭園築造の話が植治のもとに舞い込んだのは1894年の夏ごろと推測される。

平安神宮所蔵『土木部・園芸書類』に残る1894年11月21日付けの「園芸着手の件」という書類には、「園芸費千七百三円五十六銭別紙見積書ヲ以テ、着手セントス。但、工事ハ小川治兵衞ヘ特命スルモノトス」と記され、植治の作成した見積と見積書に対応する平面図・鳥瞰図が付されている。このとき築造されるのは現在の西神苑と中神苑であるが、池水の水源は琵琶湖疏水。池自体が社殿の防火用水の役割を期待されたものであった。

植治の動きは素早かった。11月28日には、「桃山官林」に残る伏見城の遺構と考えられる庭園跡の庭石の払下げ願いを平安奠都千年紀念祭協賛会から所轄の大坂営林区署に提出。価格・数量等に関

which was a five-eighths scale copy of the ancient great audience hall of the Heian-kyō Palace. The column raising ceremony was held in 1894, and it was probably in the summer of 1894 that Ueji was asked about undertaking construction of the shrine gardens.

The present West and Middle gardens were built using stones from the site of the Fushimi castle in the Momoyama state forest and water from the Lake Biwa Canal for the pond. The pond was to serve as fire protection for the shrine buildings.

する交渉を経て、翌年4月15日には払下げの許可を受けることになる。少ない予算と限られた工期、さらにあまり経験のなかったであろう様々な手続き。こうした困難な状況のなかで、植治は大工事をやり遂げる。いわば公共工事であったこの仕事の成功によって、植治に対する行政側の信頼感は増大し、1897年（明治30）の帝国京都博物館、1904年の京都府庁、さらには1913年の円山公園改良といった公共造園に植治がたずさわる契機となる。

平安神宮に話を戻すと、1911年（明治44）から1916年（大正5）には東神苑が築造される。東山を借景としたおおらかな池庭であるが、東から流れ込む渓流のデザインなどには植治らしさが光る。東神苑の築造に際し、植治は琵琶湖疏水の舟運を利用して琵琶湖西岸の志賀町守山などから大量の庭石を搬入する。疏水沿いの岡崎という平安神宮の立地を十二分に活かした材料調達であった。

また、現在の平安神宮神苑を代表する景の一つとなっている中神苑の臥龍橋は、豊臣秀吉築造の五条大橋と三条大橋の橋桁・橋脚を京都市と京都府から、それぞれ1907年（明治40）と1912-13年（大正2）に払下げを受けたものである。

このように、平安神宮神苑は京都の歴史の蓄積と風土を縦糸に、琵琶湖疏水や行政との関係といった近代の構造を横糸に、植治が見事に織りなした作品である。

構造化された植治の庭

平安神宮神苑と無鄰庵庭園の成功により、植治の声価は飛躍的に高まる。平安神宮神苑が植治の公共事業への進出の基盤となったことは前述のとおりであり、彼の仕事の幅と厚みを増すうえで重要な位置を占めることはいうまでもない。一方、無鄰庵庭園で山縣の好尚とデザインを自家薬籠中のものとした植治は、東山の翠巒のもと、琵琶湖疏水の水に恵まれた岡崎・南禅寺一帯で、それを構造化し、新興有産階級を施主として多くの庭園を

水圧を利用して水を噴き出す流れ蹲踞〈何有荘〉
A washbasin set in the stream in Kaiu-sō garden

After Ueji's success despite a tight budget, limited time allotted for construction and a lack of experience dealing with red tape, he was offered numerous other public works projects, such as the Imperial Museum of Kyoto in 1897, the Kyoto Prefectural Office in 1904, and the modification of Maruyama Park in 1913.

During the period from 1911 to 1916, Ueji returned to Heian-jingū and constructed the East Garden. It is a magnificent pond garden borrowing the scenery of the Higashiyama hills. The stream coming from the east is designed in a way that is characteristic of Ueji. When building the East Garden, Ueji brought in numerous stones

沢飛石の要などに
植治が好んで使った形の石
Ueji liked to use stones of that shape in the stream

産み出すことになる。

　京都の町人出身でフランス留学を経験し、軍服に用いるカーキ染色の成功で財を成した稲畑勝太郎の和楽庵（現・何有荘）。東京に京呉服問屋を開き京都に仕入店を開くというシステムで財を成した近江商人市田弥一郎の對龍山荘。岡崎・南禅寺一帯の高級住宅地としての可能性に着目して不動産事業を展開した近江商人塚本与三次の屋敷（現在の織宝苑・清流亭）。京都の公家徳大寺家から住友家に入り住友財閥の総帥となった十五代住友吉左衛門（春翠）の有芳園。大正期の実業界の巨頭野村徳七（得庵）の碧雲荘。熊本藩主の末裔細川護立の怡園。

　明治後期から昭和初期にかけて、それぞれの時代において成功を収めた階層が求めた空間はいかなるものであったのか。それらを如実に伝えているのが、今に残るこれらの庭園なのである。そして、東山山麓の立地と環境を最大限に活かし、琵琶湖疏水の豊かな水を躍動的に演出し、洗練された美意識と確固たる技術を基盤にしつつも、作意はあくまで表に出さない姿勢。植治の姿勢がそこにあった。

　植治は、1918年（大正7）に東京の西園寺公望邸、村井吉兵衞邸、古河虎之助邸の造園を皮切りに、以後、東は東京から西は山口まで、全国的な展開を見せる。これには公共造園で培われた造園業「植治」としてのシステムが大きく寄与したものと考えられ、それぞれの庭園では、施主の求める空間が創り出されていったのである。さはさりながら、植治の庭園の真髄を示すのが、やはり京都南禅寺・岡崎の邸宅・別荘群の庭園であることは、衆目の一致するところであろう。

　1933年（昭和8）12月2日、「植治」こと七代目小川治兵衞永眠。日本の近代をリードした政治家・実業家の求めた空間を十二分に理解し、造り手としてそれを共有するという、日本近代史のなかでも稀に見る大きさを持つ生涯であった。

1) 田辺朔郎　琵琶湖疏水の設計者（1861-1944）。工部大学校在学中に北垣国道京都府知事の依頼を受けて疏水計画を卒業論文にまとめ、卒業と同時に京都府に。欧米から招いた技師が不可能とするなか、1885年に自ら指揮して工事に着手、1890年に完成。その間、アメリカのアスペンの水力発電を視察し、疏水を利用して蹴上発電所を設置。水道、道路、市電の京都市三大事業にも参画。
2) 青蓮院宮　青蓮院宮尊融親王（1824-91）のこと。幕末期の宮廷政治家で伏見宮邦家親王の第4子。武芸の修練を積み、孝明天皇の厚い信任を受けたが安政の大獄で退隠永蟄居の処分を受ける。王政復古後は久邇宮朝彦王となる。昭和天皇の皇后の祖父。青蓮院宮の不遇の時代に、並河は生活のために七宝をはじめた。
3) 山天　天端が平らな「平天」の反意語。上部が山状に尖った形状のこと。

from Moriyama, Lake Biwa, making the most of Heian Jingū's proximity to the canal by using it for transportation.

One of the main scenic points in the Heian-Jingū gardens today is the Garyū-kyō Bridge in the Middle Garden. Ueji built the bridge using piers and girders from the Sanjō and Gojō bridges originally constructed by the warlord TOYOTOMI Hideyoshi.

The gardens of the Heian-Jingū Shrine are works woven exquisitely by Ueji, with Kyoto's climate and its years of history as the warp and the Lake Biwa Canal and other modern elements as the weft.

Ueji's Structured Gardens

With the success of the Heian-Jingū gardens and Murin-an garden, Ueji's reputation soared. As mentioned above, the Heian Jingū gardens served as a basis for his entry into public works. In addition, those gardens were significant in that they allowed him to widen and deepen his work. Furthermore, the Murin-an garden allowed him to master YAMAGATA's preferences and design sense. Subsequently, in the Okazaki area at the foot of the Higashiyama hills and well supplied with canal water, Ueji integrated his acquired knowledge, producing many gardens for clients of the emerging propertied class.

What did successful people of the late Meiji, Taishō and early Shōwa periods require for their residential gardens? They wanted to make the most of the location and environment at the foot of the Higashiyama hills and to use the abundant canal water to produce a sense of vibrancy. It was an attitude of refraining from overt contrivance, although the designs were based on skill and a sophisticated aesthetic sense. The gardens Ueji constructed are still appreciated today and are a testament to his technical and aesthetic skill.

In 1918, Ueji undertook several landscaping projects in Tokyo, after which his business became a nation-wide success.

The seventh OGAWA Jihei, or Ueji, passed away on December 2, 1933. He had a thorough understanding of what the leading politicians and businessmen of modern Japan desired for their residential spaces and shared in it as their creator. His life was a rare and magnificent one in modern Japanese history.

五感で味わう庭——植治の感性表現と意匠

尼﨑博正　京都造形芸術大学教授／日本庭園・歴史遺産研究センター所長

日本の庭園史上、特筆すべき造園家が三人いる。中世の夢窓国師、近世の小堀遠州、そして近代庭園の先覚者、植治こと七代目小川治兵衞である。彼らは独自の自然観、美意識、造形感覚を提示しつつ、新しい時代を切り拓いていったという共通点をもつ。

なかでも、プランナー、デザイナーであるとともに現場の技術者でもあった植治の存在は特異である。それは立地的特性の読み取りから、空間構成、細部意匠、施工技術にいたるまで、一貫して彼の意図を感じ取ることができるからにほかならない。植治の作庭手法の妙味を垣間見てみよう。

水と石の魔術師

せせらぎの奏でる軽快な水音に誘われて庭に降り立つ。流れを沢飛び*で渡るとき、躍動的な水の動きが直接足下に伝わってくる。その臨場感あふれる心地よさは、まるで己が庭の一部になったような錯覚に陥ってしまうほど。

このような水の魔術師としての植治の才覚の片鱗は、「無鄰庵」で山縣有朋と出会う直前に作庭した並河靖之七宝記念館の庭園ですでに発揮されていた。

1894年（明治27）11月15日に行われた竣工披露の様子を伝える翌日の「日出新聞」[1)]は「並川氏新宅落成」と題して、独創的な一文字縁先手水鉢（27ページ参照）の設えなどとともに「棗形の水鉢をめぐりて池水を吐出せしむる造作は尤も好意匠にして……」と、そのさりげなくも非凡な水の扱いに注目している。

ちなみに、のちの植治を彷彿とさせるもう一つの要素として、座敷から池の水面を通して粟田山を望む軸線の存在も見逃せない。無鄰庵をはじめとする南禅寺界隈の別荘庭園群でみられるように、東山と一体となった雄大な空間構成は植治の庭の根幹をなしていたからである。

無鄰庵で近代造園に目覚めた植治は、山縣の求めに応じて、あたかも東山の裾から流れ落ちてくるかのように三段の滝を設えた。杉木立からほとばしり出た水は浅い水面にモミジを映しこみ、芝生の起伏を縫うようにして座敷前へと導かれ

尼﨑博正（あまさき・ひろまさ）植治研究の第一人者。1946年、兵庫県に生まれる。京都大学農学部卒業。農学博士。研究者であるとともに自ら作庭や文化財庭園の保存・修復に取り組む。文化庁文化審議会専門委員など多くの公職を務める。主な著書に『植治の庭─小川治兵衛の世界』、『石と水の意匠─植治の造園技術』、『市中の山居─尼崎博正作庭集』などがある。

Gardens for All Five Senses
—Ueji's Design Insights

AMASAKI Hiromasa
Professor at the Kyoto University of Art and Design.
Director of the Research Center for Japanese Garden Art and Historical Heritage

There have been three notable landscape architects in Japanese landscaping history: Musō Kokushi of the medieval period, KOBORI Enshū of the premodern period, and Ueji, or the seventh OGAWA Jihei, the pioneer of modern Japanese gardens. They were similar in that each began a new age with his original view of nature, aesthetic sense, and formative insights. However, Ueji was perhaps the greatest of the three. He was a planner, a designer, and at the same time, a field technician. From his way of grasping the features of a site, spatial organization, design details, and construction techniques it is always possible to perceive his intent. The following is a glimpse into Ueji's exquisite landscaping technique.

A Master Magician with Water and Stone

You hear the rhythmic babble of a stream as you stand in the garden. Walking across the stream on stepping stones, you intuitively sense the flow of the water past your feet. In its calming presence, you have the illusion of being a part of the garden itself.

Ueji was a master of water. His talent manifested itself early on, in the construction of the Namikawa Cloisonné Museum of Kyoto garden, just before he met YAMAGATA Aritomo at Murin-an.

A local paper reported on the completion ceremony, held on November 15, 1894. Under the heading "Namikawa's New House Completed" the newspaper noted Ueji's unusual yet unobtrusive use of water, "the best part of the design is the water passing through an oval washbasin and flowing into the pond," as well as his innovative washbasin arrangement (see p. 27).

In this garden, there is another element that anticipates Ueji's later works. It is the view from the reception room of the Higashiyama hills, reflected in the pond surface. Ueji's magnificent

Amasaki Hiromasa: Born in 1946 in Hyogo Prefecture. Graduated from the Faculty of Agriculture, Kyoto University. He is a researcher and at the same time he pursues landscaping and is involved in preservation of gardens designated as cultural properties. He is also active publicly, for example, as an expert member of the Council for Cultural Affairs, Agency for Cultural Affairs.

流れにリズムと水音をつくる瀬落ち〈無鄰庵〉
A weir in the Murin-an garden

る。瀬落ち*から絶え間なく発せられる水の響きが別世界を演出するという巧妙さ。従来の日本庭園が、歌に詠まれた名所の風景をモチーフとしてきたのに対して、植治は身近かな自然、誰もが見覚えのある田園や里山の風景を原寸で描き出そうとしたのである。その表現は近代という時代が求めた自然観を反映したものであり、「歌枕の庭園化」からの脱皮を意味していた。それはまた、「眺める庭」から「五感で味わう庭」への転換といってもよいだろう。

さて、右方から一段目を落とし、左へ振って次の一段を、そして再び右へ流して最後の水落ちとする無鄰庵の滝石組（37ページ参照）は、醍醐寺「三宝院」のそれから学んだものにちがいない。植治の三段の滝への執着はことのほか強く、「碧雲荘庭園」ではスケールを大幅にアップし、さらに亡くなる直前の1933年に作庭した都ホテル「葵殿庭園」では斜面全体を三段の滝でまとめ上げるまでに展開するのである。

流れの中に瀬落ちをつくり、あるいは川床に小石を埋め込むなどして水の動きに変化をもたせる手法も見事というほかない。たとえば建築家・武田五一[2]の設計で1913年に着工し、翌年に完了した円山公園、その自然の渓谷を思わせるリズミカルな流れは植治の感性の豊かさと技の確かさを髣髴とさせる。それは近代日本庭園の意匠を公共の場に顕現させたという点においても画期的であった。

水とともに庭の骨格をなす素材といえば石である。琵琶湖疏水の舟運に目をつけた植治は、琵琶湖西岸に産する「守山石」*を大量に京都に運び込んだ。いわゆる産地直送である。これによって大規模造園工事に対応できる体制が整ったといってよい。さらに、1899年に綾部まで鉄道が敷かれると丹波方面の庭石を、1910年の山陰本線開通以後は日本海側に産する緑色凝灰岩を搬入するという機敏さであった。

このように植治は、京都の伝統的な庭石であるチャート*や鞍馬石*、貴船石*といったブランド品にこだわることなく、大量に入手が可能な庭石の特徴、たとえば守山石の褶曲した層理に目をつけ、その扱い方で勝負したことがわかる。

一方で植治は、加工石による独自のデザインを提示している。沢飛びに臼石などの加工石を用いることによって自然と人工の対比を際立たせる独自の美意識、その極致が無隣庵を作庭中に手がけた平安神宮の中神苑にある「臥龍橋」（43ページ参照）である。架け替え工事で不要となった三条大橋と五条大橋の橋脚・橋桁の払い下げを受け、いわば廃材を用いて、かくのごとく斬新なデザインを成し遂げた植治の力量がただものではないことを

organization of space, incorporating the Higashiyama hills into his gardens, is the essential feature of his garden-designs, as seen in Murin-an and other villa gardens scattered in the vicinity of Nanzen-ji Temple.

Ueji's next project, the Murin-an garden built for YAMAGATA Aritomo, provided him with several insights into modern landscaping. At YAMAGATA's request, Ueji set up a three-level waterfall that gives the impression of starting from the foot of the Higashiyama hills. Water trickling out from amongst cedar trees forms a shallow pool whose surface reflects maples. The water then flows toward the reception room through an undulating lawn and over a weir. The constant sound of water is an ingenious way to create the sense of being in another world. Traditional Japanese gardens were constructed in imitation of some scenic spot depicted in poetry. In contrast, Ueji's insights led him to represent, in full size, familiar natural landscapes that everyone knew. His manner of expression was influenced by a modern view of nature and implied departure from the clichéd reproduction of poem scenery. It was in a sense a shift from gardens for contempla-

川床に小石を埋め込んだ流れ〈無鄰庵〉
The stream in the Murin-an garden

波打つ縞目の守山石を用いた三段の滝の一部〈ウェスティン都ホテル〉
A threadlike waterfall in the Aoiden garden at Westin Miyako Kyoto

示す作品といえよう。

開放的な露地空間

　流れを主体とした水の躍動的な表現は、植治のデザインの奥深さを示すとともに、茶の湯の空間に新たな境地をもたらすものでもあった。植治の露地*はじつに開放的で、従来の露地のイメージを一新したといってよい。茶室の傍らで軽快な水音をたてる流れの岸辺には蛇籠*が伏せられ、カワラナデシコやキキョウが四季折々の風情を感じさせてくれる。その流れの中に据えられた手水鉢から清水が溢れ出る様はじつに瑞々しい。「流れ蹲踞」*である。

　碧雲荘を訪れてみよう。広大な園池を有する大庭園に巧みに組み込まれた露地空間、大寄せの茶会にも対応できる仕組みだ。茶会のときには不老門（兜門）から入って寄付きの「龍頭軒」へ、そしてアカマツとモミジの木漏れ日をうけながら茶室へと向かう。右手に見えるのが広間の「花泛亭」、左方の流れに目をやると岸近くの水面に小さな手水鉢*が浮かんでいる（76ページ参照）。この流れ蹲踞で手と口を清めるのだが、身をかがめると土橋の桁下から大池の水面とオーバーフローする水の動きが眼前に迫ってくる。そればかりではない。ふと上方へと視線を移すと、遥か彼方に比叡の山がくっきりと浮かび上がっているではないか。

　このような意外性の演出も植治の得意とするところで、つねに意表をつく趣向に、訪れる者は心地よい驚きを感じる。このように、植治の露地は全五感を働かせて味わう庭への発想の転換をもたらしたといえる。

　無鄰菴の滝石組は、三段になった滝の流れの向きを各段で変える見事な仕掛けだ（37ページ参照）。この構成は植治が醍醐寺三宝院で学んだものに違いない。三段の滝に対する植治の思い入れは強く、碧雲荘の大規模な三段の滝をつくり上げ、さらには没年の1933年直前に作庭した都ホテル葵殿庭園では、庭全体の斜面を支配する三段の滝を構築した。

　水の流れに変化をつける手法も見事で、浅瀬や玉石の埋め込みなどは、その典型だ。たとえば、建築家の武田五一[1]が設計し、1913年に工事が始まり1914年に竣工した円山公園では、リズム感のある水の流れが自然の渓流のようで、植治の豊かな想像力と卓越した技を示している。これは近代日本の造園を公共空間にもたらした画期的な作品であった。

　石は水と並んで庭づくりの中心的な素材である。琵琶湖疏水による運搬の便を活かして、琵琶湖西岸の産地から守山石を直接京都に大量に運び込み、大規模な作庭を可能にした。さらに1899年に鉄道が綾部まで延びると丹波方面の石を京都に運ばせ、1910年に山陰線が開通するとすぐに日本海側の青石などを搬入しはじめた。行動の早い人物であった。

　植治は京都の庭園で伝統的に用いられてきたチャート、鞍馬石、貴船石といった「銘石」にこだわらず、豊富に入手できるものを利用し、守山石の畳み込まれた地層のような特徴を最大限に活かした。

　植治独自のデザインの工夫のひとつは、加工石の取り入れだった。自然物と人工物との対比を際立たせる独特な美意識を持ち、石臼を飛石に用いたことなどに見ることができる。究極の例は、無鄰菴を作庭中に手がけた平安神宮の中神苑にある臥龍橋（43ページ参照）で

tion to gardens for appreciation with all five senses.

The waterfall stone arrangement at Murin-an drives the water flow so that it's direction changes at each of the three levels (see p. 37). There is no doubt that Ueji learned this arrangement at Daigo-ji Sambō-in temple. He had a strong attachment to three-level waterfalls. He created a large-scale three-level waterfall in the Hekiun-sō garden. Moreover, in 1933, immediately before his death, he constructed the Miyako Hotel Aoiden garden, where a three level waterfall governs the garden's entire slope.

He exhibited exquisite technique in producing variation in the flow of water, with the creation of shallows and the embedding of pebbles in streambeds as just two examples. Take for instance Maruyama Park, designed by architect TAKEDA Goichi[1], the construction of which commenced in 1913 and was completed in 1914. The rhythmic flow of water is like that in a natural mountain stream, demonstrating Ueji's rich imagination and superb skill. It was an epoch-making work, in that it brought modern Japanese landscape design to a public space.

Stones are a material as central to garden-design as water. Taking advantage of transportation by the Lake Biwa Canal, Ueji imported to Kyoto many Moriyama stones directly from their source on the western shore of Lake Biwa. This enabled him to undertake large-scale landscaping projects. Furthermore, when the railroad reached Ayabe in 1899, he brought stones produced in the Tamba area to Kyoto, and in 1910 when the San-in line opened he began to bring in stones, such as green tuff, from areas along the Sea of Japan. He was a man who was quick to act.

Ueji was not particular about "brand-name" stones such as the chert, Kurama, and Kibune that were traditionally used in Kyoto gardens. He used whatever was available in abundance and made the most of specific features, such as the folded strata of Moriyama stones.

One of Ueji's unique design innovations was the incorporation of shaped stones. He had a unique aesthetic feel for producing marked contrasts between natural and artificial objects, which can be seen in his use of millstones as stepping-stones. The ultimate example is the Garyū-kyō Bridge (see p. 43) in the Middle Garden at Heian-Jingū, which he built while constructing Murin-

15

とするところであった。

小間の茶室「又隠」の内露地*のデザインも大胆そのものである。1924年2月19日、益田鈍翁とともに碧雲荘に招かれた近代数寄者・高橋箒庵3)は、その想像を絶する「降り蹲踞」*を目にしたときの心境を次のように述べている。

「一方の小高き丘腹より流れ出づる水を先ず水盤に受けて、之を酒造家用の細長き石樋に移し、其水を更に青竹の樋に落として蹲踞に代用した、其趣向は左る事ながら当荘の如き規模雄大なる茶席の露地に、斯かる衒奇なる細工が調和すべきや、茶人の批評は如何あろうと思われた」。(『甲子大正茶道記』)

また、露地の構成についても、「或は園遊会などに利用せんとする茶事以外の考慮があって彼が如く開放的に構造せられた者かもしれぬが、茶庭の原則を無視した痕跡が少なくないようである」と手厳しい。裏を返せば、植治の自由奔放なデザイン感覚にさすがの箒庵も脱帽した様子をみてとることができよう。

周辺景観の庭園化

自由奔放なデザインもさることながら、碧雲荘の圧巻は何といっても「待月軒」から広大な園池を通して東山を望む雄大な景観である。

同1924年11月14日、再び碧雲荘を訪れた箒庵は「碧雲荘は東面して右手に近く南禅寺を控え、永観堂鹿ケ谷より黒谷に至る三十六峰の大部分を一眸中に収め、庭前に大池を湛えて其周囲に亭台庵室を配置した結構、真に風雅幽清を極めて居る」(『甲子大正茶道記』)と記している。

植治の庭の本質は自然的・文化的景観を含めた周辺環境との融合にあるといっても過言ではない。アカマツを数多く植栽したのも、東山の自然景観との連続性を意識してのことであった。1934年に京都を襲った室戸台風の被害をうけるまで、東山は赤い幹が夕日に映えて美しいアカマツ林が優先していたからである。

それは17世紀前半に確立された借景の手法のように、生垣や築地塀*など人工の見切り線を入れ、自然景観を庭園内の景と対峙させることによって弁証法的に生け捕ろうというのではない。よりスケールの大きい融合の思想が根底にあるとみるべきであろう。

東山の中腹にポツンとたたずむ永観堂の多宝塔も、じつは植治の意図したものにほかならない。彼は自然景観のなかに点在する人工物、すなわち南禅寺の山門や黒谷の塔などの歴史的建造物を眺望対象として積極的に取り込もうとした。宮島の厳島神社や琵琶湖岸の浮御堂などの例をあげるまでもなく、人工物を付加することによって周辺の自然景観が庭園化されることを植治はよく知っていたにちがいない。

このような東山を仰ぎ見る南禅寺界隈の別荘庭園群と趣を異にしているのが、清水二年坂の高台寺土井(旧清水吉次郎の別荘・十牛庵)である。霊山の麓に位置するこの庭園は、斜面を利用して「山上より小渓を作り瀧を象とり池に注ぐ設計」(『京華林泉帖』)4)もさることながら、「晴時は大阪を望む」絶景の地であり、眼下の八坂の塔と京都市街を俯瞰眺望の主景としているところに特徴がある。

an. He used piers and girders from the Sanjō and Gojō bridges which had been discarded by the government at the time those bridges were replaced. Ueji used these materials to realize a completely novel design. The Garyū-kyō Bridge is another work that reveals his extraordinary ability.

Open Spaces for Tea Gardens

Ueji used flows of water as a means of expressing vibrancy. His use of water, indicative of the depth of his design sense, added a novel aspect to tea gardens. Ueji transformed the conventional image of tea gardens and created truly open spaces. A stream flows rhythmically past a tearoom. Gabions are placed along the stream banks where wild pinks and balloon flowers bring seasonal changes to the scenery. A washbasin placed in a stream continually overflows with fresh water that is truly invigorating.

At Hekiun-sō, open spaces are ingeniously incorporated in the huge garden with its large pond. It is designed to accommodate a large number of guests for tea ceremony. For a tea ceremony, you enter the garden through the Furo gate, pass by the Ryūzu-ken tearoom at the gateway, and, in dappled sunshine filtering through red pines and maples, approach the tearoom. On your right is the Kahen-tei tearoom. On your left is a stream. A small washbasin is placed over the stream close to the bank (see p. 76). As you stoop over the basin to wash your hands and rinse your mouth, you have a close up view of the surface of the large pond, and below the supports of an earthen bridge a weir overflowing with water. Moreover, when you gaze upward, you have a clear view of distant Mount Hiei. Ueji was skilled at producing pleasant surprises like that.

Ueji's design for the small Yushiki tearoom garden was very bold. On February 19, 1924, TAKAHASHI Sōan[2] was invited to Hekiun-sō. A critic of modern times TAKAHASHI saw the washbasin built unthinkably below ground level and had the following reaction:

"Water flows out of one side of a mound into a flower bowl, then into a long and hollowed-out stone. The water then flows down to a green bamboo gutter and this is intended as a washbasin. Putting aside the design itself, I wonder whether such an eccentric piece as this suits the tea garden of this magnificent villa. I would really

その構図は華頂山を背にし、斜面に三段の滝を設えた都ホテルの「葵殿庭園」も同じである。葵殿から北を望めば、遥か遠くに比叡山から北山の山並みが、中景に黒谷の尖塔が、そして近くは南禅寺・岡崎一帯の町並みが手に取れる。1890年4月8日、琵琶湖疏水の開通式が催される前日に開設された吉水園を前身とする土地柄ならではのことである。

　また「南禅寺疏水水道の下天授庵の南にあり山峡を包ねて……」と『京華林泉帖』に記された何有荘（もと稲畑勝太郎氏の「和楽庵」）の眺望景観も圧巻である。書院の正面に滔々と流れ落ちる「瑞龍の滝」（58ページ参照）が紅葉に映える情景の素晴らしさもさることながら、上方の「草堂」に昇れば、眼下に南禅寺の山門、遥か彼方に比叡山から北山の山並み、さらには愛宕山までが一望のもとにあり、修学院離宮「隣雲亭」からの眺望に匹敵する雄大な世界がパノラマのように展開しているのである。

　庭は「壮大な自然の輪廻」と「創造的な人の営み」との融合にほかならない。植治の庭はその極意を如実に物語っているといえよう。

1）「日出新聞」「京都新聞」の前身。
2）**武田五一** アール・ヌーボーを日本に紹介した建築家 (1872-1938年)。円山公園や何有荘（旧和楽庵）の建築を担当した。
3）**益田鈍翁**は三井物産創始者で本名・孝、**高橋箒庵**は三越初代社長で本名・義雄、**野村得庵**は野村財閥の創始者で本名・徳七。明治の富裕層の多くは美術品などの収集家としても知られ、3人は碧雲荘で会う5年前には共同購入した「佐竹本・三十六歌仙絵巻」を切断して分けあった仲間でもある。
4）『京華林泉帖』湯本文彦が編集し1909年に京都府庁が発行。当時の庭の事情を写真と解説とで紹介している。

like to hear what tea masters have to say."

TAKAHASHI had something else to say about the composition of the tea garden: "I am aware that this garden is open so that it may be used for purposes other than tea ceremony, say for a garden party, but I see more than a few signs that the principles of a tearoom garden have been ignored." In fact, TAKAHASHI's remark suggests that he took his hat off to Ueji's free-spirited design sense.

Surrounding Scenery Brought into the Garden

Aside from the unbridled design, at Hekiun-sō garden the noble sight of the Higashiyama hills viewed over the large garden pond must not be missed.

On November 14, 1924, TAKAHASHI Sōan visited Hekiun-sō again. "Facing east, Hekiun-sō commands most of the thirty-six Higashiyama hills, from nearby Nanzen-ji Temple to the right, through Eikan-dō, Shishigatani and Kurotani to the left. The large, serene garden pond is surrounded by a deliberate arrangement of huts and arbors. Here I see the ultimate example of refinement and subtlety."

The essence of Ueji's landscape art, I believe, is the integration between his gardens and their surroundings, including both natural and cultural characteristics. He frequently used red cedars, with the aim of producing continuity between the garden and the natural scenery of Higashiyama. Red cedar trees were dominant on Higashiyama and their red trunks shone beautifully in the sunset, until they were damaged by the Muroto Typhoon of 1934.

In the first half of the seventeenth century, the technique known as "*shakkei*" (borrowed scenery) was established in order to pair natural scenery with a garden, or to capture the natural scenery for the garden, using man-made partition lines such as hedges and roofed earthen walls. Ueji's technique was not traditional *shakkei*. His works must have stemmed from a more profound understanding of integration.

The Eikan-dō pagoda stands alone on the Higashiyama hillside. Ueji purposely integrated it into the Hekiun-sō garden (see p. 75). He did not hesitate to incorporate the artificial objects scattered throughout a natural setting as part of the view he wished to create: historic buildings such as the main gate of Nanzen-ji Temple and the pagoda of Kurotani for instance. Ueji must have fully understood that the surrounding natural scenery turns into a garden if a man-made structure is introduced, as seen with the Itsukushima Shinto Shrine on Miyajima and the Ukimidō floating temple on Lake Biwa.

Villa gardens in the vicinity of Nanzen-ji Temple commanding a view of the Higashiyama hills can be contrasted with Kōdaiji-Doi at Kiyomizu Ninenzaka. Situated at the foot of a sacred hill and making use of the natural slope, this garden has a small stream, which descends from the hilltop and flows into a pond as a waterfall. Moreover, it has as its main feature an exquisite view of the city of Kyoto, which even extends to Osaka on sunny days.

The same composition is present in the Aoi-den Garden at Westin Miyako Kyoto Hotel, which is backed by the Kachō hill and has a three-level waterfall on its slope. From Aoi-den, you will see Mount Hiei and Mount Kitayama far to the north, the steeple of Kurotani in the middle distance, and the houses of the Nanzen-ji and Okazaki area nearby. The Miyako Hotel opened on this site, on April 8, 1890, one day before the opening ceremony of the canal between Kyoto and Lake Biwa.

In addition, the splendid view from Kaiu-sō cannot be missed. The abundant flow of the Zuiryū waterfall (see p. 58) in front of the guest room is wonderful when seen in autumn colors. Moreover, as you climb up to the thatch roofed tearoom, you will enjoy a panoramic view of the Nanzen-ji main gate below, the far off Mount Hiei, Mount Kita-yama, and also Mount Atago-yama. It is an impressive view comparable to that from the Rinun-tei pavilion of Shūgaku-in Rikyū.

A garden is the result of integration between the marvelous transitions of Nature and human creative activity. Regarding this magic formula, Ueji's landscape art speaks for itself.

1. TAKEDA Goichi (1872-1928): architect. TAKEDA introduced "art nouveau" to Japan. He was in charge of the design of Maruyama Park and the building of Kaiu-sō.
2. TAKAHASHI Sōan was the first president of Mitukoshi, Ltd. Wealthy Japanese people of the Meiji period are known to have been great masters of tea ceremony and avid art collectors.

並河靖之七宝記念館庭園

京都市東山区三条通北裏白川筋東入る堀池町388
1894年作庭／340m²（約103坪）／施主・並河靖之

池庭の泉水は
床の下まで潜み込み、
水に浮かぶがごとき世界
をつくる。自然につつまれ、
自然に溶けこむことで、
人は心のやすらぎを覚える。
現存するもっとも初期の作品で、
その後の植治を彷彿させる
若き日の挑戦作

並河靖之七宝記念館は、明治・大正期に活躍した七宝家で帝室技芸員を務めた並河靖之の旧宅と工房、窯場を公開する。家と庭は1894年の完成。表は京格子や虫籠窓をそなえた京町家の表屋づくりで、背後に二階建ての主家がつづく。京町家と書院ふうの二つの様式が併存する。

欧米で高い評価を得た並河のもとには、英国のエドワード皇太子をはじめ外国の賓客が多く訪れたことから、和室の応接室には椅子やテーブルが置かれ、鴨居も高い。

七宝制作に必要な施設を建てて残った空間に、隣家に住んでいた若き植治が庭をつくった。小規模の庭は別として、植治の処女作とされる。

敷地は狭いが、七宝制作のために引かれた琵琶湖疏水の水を利用し、植治は大きな池をつくることにした。南禅寺の境内を抜けて疏水の水を西に運ぶ水路閣が1888年に完成し、1893年には円山公園の噴水が人びとを驚嘆させたが、庭の完成はその翌年のことである。個人の邸宅の庭に疏水の水を用いた初めての例となった。二階建ての主屋をその池の上に張り出させ、建物と庭とを一体化させる釣殿的構成を植治はあみだした。

斬新な「水の庭」で注目を浴びた植治は、つづいて無鄰庵の作庭にとりかかる。

1　玄関わきにさりげなく据えられた石を飾る緑
Standing stone in the entrance

2 門をくぐると小さな庭が待ち受ける。
直線的な構成に植物と敷石とが調和する
The stone pavemant and an ornamantal stone in the entrance

Namikawa Cloisonné Museum of Kyoto Garden

The Namikawa Cloisonné Museum of Kyoto is the former house and atelier of NAMIKAWA Yasuyuki, a ceramic artist of the Meiji and Taishō eras. The building and garden were completed in 1894. From the street, the one-story entrance looks like a traditional Kyoto townhouse but behind it stands a modern two-storied wooden building. NAMIKAWA received many foreign guests as shown by a table and chairs unusually placed on the mats of the Japanese-style reception room.

The young Ueji, who was living next door, created the garden. It is said that this was his first work. Ueji designed a big pond using water from the Lake Biwa Canal. NAMIKAWA's residence was the first place where water from the Lake Biwa Canal was used for a private garden.

3 沓脱石から庭へとつづく飛び石は雨に濡れている。大きく丸い石は柱の礎石に使われる伽藍石
On one side of the reception room, the stepping stones leads into a dense garden

4　雨の翌日。池に張り出した主屋が、敷地の狭いことを気づかせない
On the other side of the reception room, the pond creates a wide-open space

施主・並河靖之（1845-1927）

武家の三男として京都に生まれた並河靖之は、門跡寺院の青蓮院宮侍臣を務める並河家に10歳で養子にはいり、のちの久邇宮朝彦親王の侍臣となる。1872年、27歳で余技として装飾陶芸である有線七宝の技法の修得に着手。やがて宮家に仕えるかたわら七宝業をはじめることになり、その4年後にはフィラデルフィア万国博覧会で銅賞受賞。その2年後のパリ万国博覧会では、銀製七宝茶入で銀賞受賞。宮家での文化的洗練と富岡鉄斎との交流が並河の美的感性を高めたのであろうか。現在では再現も難しい細密な文様と鮮やかな色彩の有線七宝の技術は、並河によって頂点を迎え、並河とともに失われた。

NAMIKAWA Yasuyuki (1845-1927)

Adopted by the NAMIKAWA family at the age of ten he worked as a valet for the Imperial Prince Kuninomiya Asahiko, in the temple of Shōren-in in Kyoto. At the age of 27 while serving the Imperial family, he started to learn the traditional ceramic technique called cloisonné. Three years later, in 1876 he received the silver prize at the Philadelphia Universal Exposition. He exhibited his work in several expositions throughout the world and received the gold prize at the Universal Exposition in Paris in 1889.

並河邸を作庭した1894年当時の植治は、まだ34歳。これほど広い庭づくりを依頼されたのは初めてだった。植治は、並河の意向を受けながら思い切ったプランを提案する。七宝制作のために取り込んだ疏水の水をたっぷりと蓄える池を軒下までうがち、室内からはあたかも水に浮かんでいるがごとき心境にさせようというのが植治の意図である。池の周囲にはたくさんの樹木を植栽し、樹種の高低差が立体感と遠近感を演出する。そのうえで、少し大きめの沢飛石*で平らな拡がりを強調するなど、大胆で優美な石づかいはその後の植治を彷彿させる。近世の寺院庭園の基本をふまえているものの、植治らしい作風と意匠は、この段階ですでにみることができる。植治の作庭の変遷を知るうえで、貴重な庭でもある。100年を超えて、深い植栽はいまや幽邃な印象を与える。

Ueji created the garden of NAMIKAWA Yasuyuki in 1894, he was only 34 years old. The very dense and dark plantation of garden trees, and the standing stones are still in the line of traditional techniques, but using water formerly drawn for the manufacturing of cloisonné ceramics, Ueji had the revolutionary idea of creating a pond. Although it is a relatively narrow garden surrounded by other townhouses, the pond creates an illusion of wide-open space. The use of water in a townhouse garden was completely innovative and water became one of the main characteristics of Ueji's future gardens. Also, the use of stepping stone crossing the pond is reminiscent of Ueji's future designs. In this sense, the garden of the Namikawa Cloisonné Museum of Kyoto is a precious window into understanding the changes that occurred in Ueji's creations.

5 池は床下にまではいりこみ、建物と一体化する。池のなかに立つ「岩島」は伝統的な手法の一つ

The pond extends under the floor creating harmony between the garden and the house

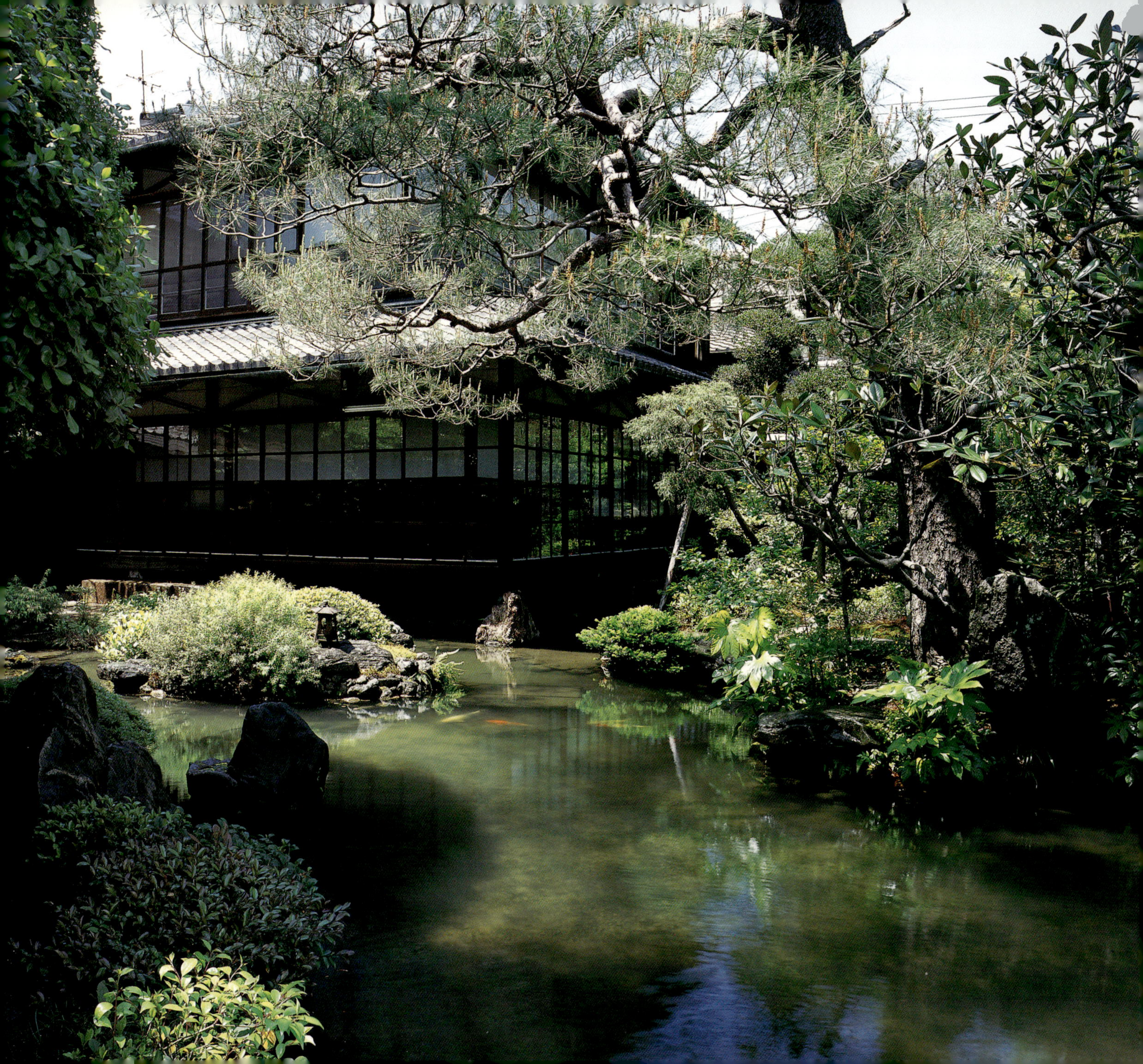

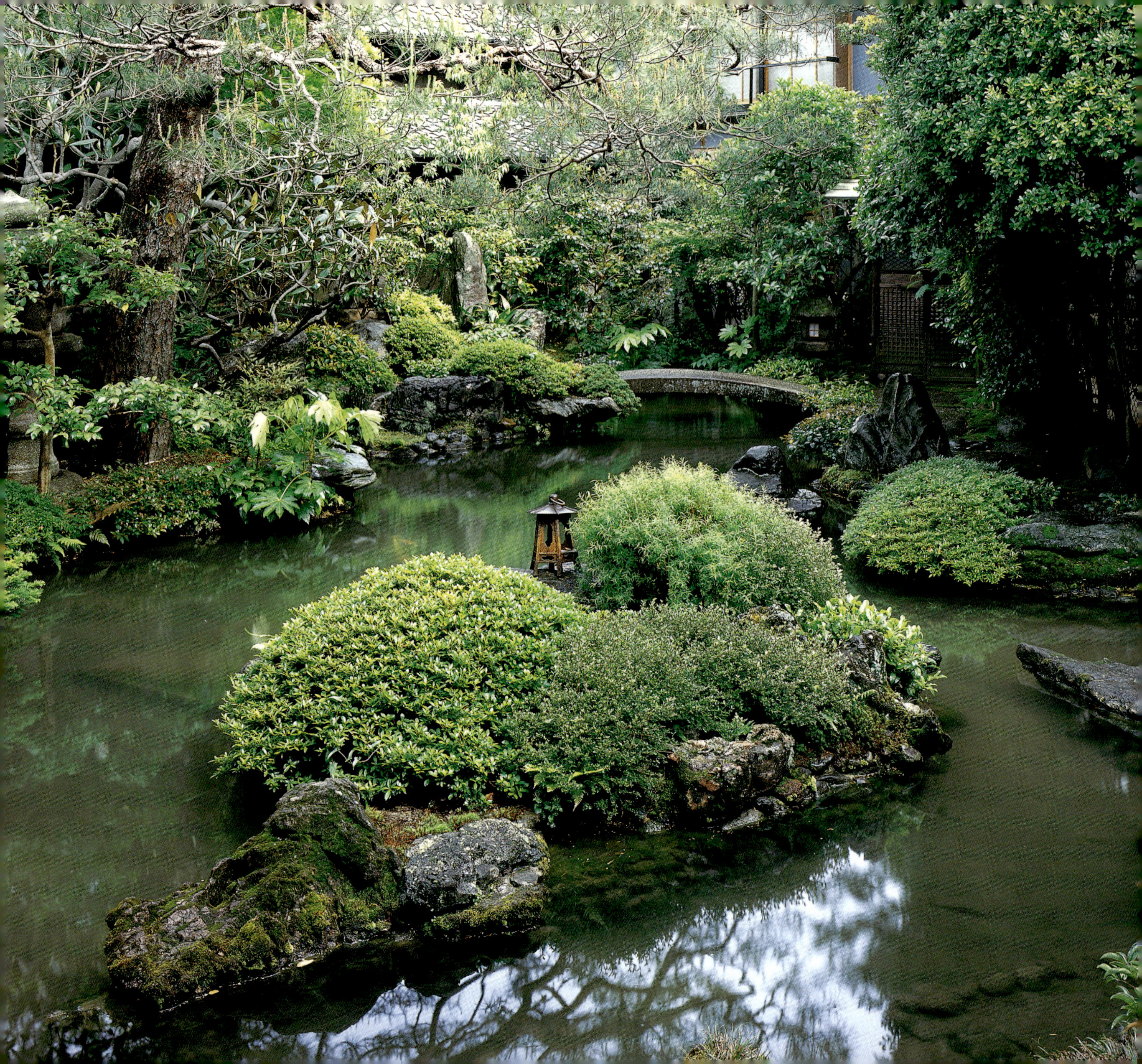

6　水と植物が「生命」の誕生を想起させる。池の奥に橋が架かるが、その向こうの石は不老不死の仙人が住む理想郷、蓬莱山を表現しているのだろうか

Standing stones behind the pond create the illusion of depth

7　池のなかを歩かせる沢飛石の巧みな配置は、その後の植治の特徴的な意匠になる

Stepping stones at the edge of the pond

並河靖之氏を屋敷に訪ぬ

明治期の美術評論家・作家　黒田天外

明治二九年、一二月八日、並河靖之氏を三条通東北裏堀池町の屋敷に訪う。

室ははなはだ雅整にして、庭園は幽邃閑寂を極め、筧水にやあらん涼然として鳴る。すこぶる、大いにけっこう、ほとんど人目を驚かすに足る。余、すなわち七宝における氏の経歴を請い問う。氏曰く、

「人間の身の上はわからぬもので、維新前には異人の首を斬ってやろうと威張った者が、今はその異人の金を取ることを商賣にするようになりました」と呵々一笑。

工場は邸内の庭続きにあり、四方は玻璃（ガラス）障子をはめ、室内清爽にして、庭園の竹樹怪石ことごとく映し通しきたり。池水また涼然として不断の音楽を奏す。まことに美術工藝家の工場と称するに足る。

業に従う者二十余人。線金を嵌するあり、蝋薬を塗るあり、色彩を和するあり、砥石にてとぐあり、工を施こすの順次により各席をなし、秩序すこぶる整々たり。その精細緻密にして、施行の繁雑なる。余をして感嘆のあまり、「七宝家には成りたくない」と思わしむ。

8　手洗いに通じる渡り廊下のあたりは
控えめで清浄なたたずまい

A washbasin stands at the edge of the
roofed passage leading to the lavatory

9　縁から庭におりるための
巨大な2本の沓脱石は、
大津の膳所城の櫓の葛石（かずらいし）
であったとか

These two shaped stones were brought
from the ruins of Zeze castle, in Shiga
prefecture

10　一文字の手水鉢は鞍馬石。
空中に浮かぶがごとく置かれている

Made of red granite rock, this washbasin
seems to play with gravity

◆ **In the garden ...**

NAMIKAWA *Yasuyuki*
interviewed by KURODA *Tengai*
in the Meiji era

"In the house, the interior design follows traditional forms. In the garden, the dense trees emanate a serene atmosphere and the water flows tumultuously. This combination surprises all my visitors." Then I asked about NAMIKAWA Yasuki's personal career in cloisonné ceramics. He laughed and answered: "The human being is inscrutable; before the Meiji Restoration, everybody wanted to cut the heads off the Westerners but now we are doing business using their money."

NAMIKAWA's atelier is located in a corner of the garden. It is surrounded by sliding doors fitted with panes of glass so it is very bright. The standing rocks and dense trees reflect on the glass and the ceaseless melody of the water can be heard from inside. This is truly the place for the atelier of an artist.

There are about 20 craftsmen working here, some working on silver, some waxing, some working on colors, some polishing jewels… each role is precisely defined and order reigns. I was in admiration before such complex and refined work but NAMIKAWA said: "Actually, I didn't want to become a cloisonné craftsman."

11 瓦と石の組み合わせは遊び心にあふれる
A refined design in stone and tile for the stone pavement that leads to the garden

12　池の中で主屋を支える根石は
　　貴船石。亀を連想させる。
　　亀が背中で家を支えて
　　蓬莱に向かう姿とも解釈できる

This rock supporting the house pillar is
reminiscent of a turtle, symbol of
longevity in traditional gardens

無鄰庵庭園

京都市左京区南禅寺草川町31
1894-96年作庭/3,135m²（約950坪）/施主・山縣有朋

2　座敷に腰をおろすと眼前に芝生の緑の空間が拡がる。
苔に代えて芝生を使うのは山縣の注文の一つ。
木々の向こうには東山がたおやかな姿をみせる

It was the idea of the owner YAMAGATA Aritomo
to use a lawn in order to create open spaces

無鄰庵は、山縣有朋が郷里・萩にしつらえた草庵の名でもある。隣家もなく閑静であったことに由来する。植治はここで山縣という師に運命的に邂逅する。旧来の寂びの庭ではなく、のびやかで開放的な植治の庭の誕生である

植治に作庭を依頼した山縣有朋は、幕末から明治・大正にかけて活躍した軍人であり政治家。よほど無鄰庵の名が気に入ったのか、1891年に首相を辞めて京都に移った山縣は、木屋町二条にある角倉了以の旧宅を別荘とし「無鄰庵」と命名。さらに翌年、南禅寺近くのこの場所に新たな「無鄰庵」をつくらせた。主屋は和風の簡素な木造二階建て。茶を好んだ山縣は武家茶道の藪内流の燕庵を模した茶室を庭内にしつらえさせ、1897年には洋館を増設した。

山縣に植治を紹介したのが、同じ長州人の久原庄三郎。植治34歳のころで、作庭経験は並河邸ぐらい。着工した1894年に日清戦争がはじまり、山縣が第一軍司令官として清国へ出征する間、工事の監督は久原に託された。山縣と久原という優れた二人のディレクターの要求に、植治はみごとに応えた。植治の評価が確立するとともに、以後、活躍の舞台がいくつも用意されることになる。無鄰庵は1941年に京都市に寄贈され、1951年には国の名勝に指定された。

1　100年をへて樹木は二階建ての主屋を凌ぐ高さに成長した
Overview of the villa. Behind the trees are hidden a tearoom and a two-storied Western-style building

Murin-an Garden

Murin-an is the name of the villa constructed by YAMAGATA Aritomo, Army General and politician of the Meiji and Taishō eras. Murin-an means the "hermitage with no neighbors," it was so called because it was first located in a very quiet area in YAMAGATA's hometown, in Yamaguchi Prefecture. YAMAGATA must have particularly liked this name because when he moved to Kyoto in 1891, he named his new villa Murin-an again, even though it was located in the center of town. One year later he moved again to the current location near the Nanzen-ji temple and constructed a new Murin-an villa. YAMAGATA drew up the general plan for the garden and gave Ueji the following conditions: create an open space with a lawn, use natural trees like firs and create streams with water from the Lake Biwa Canal. When construction started in 1894, the Japan-Chinese war began and YAMAGATA had to leave to fight. Ueji was still young and had little experience but he fulfilled and maybe even surpassed YAMAGATA's expectations. Today Murin-an is a symbol of the modern Japanese garden. It was designated a place of scenic beauty in 1951 and since then has been protected as a cultural asset.

借景の東山の麓から流れ出したかのような水の流れは、陽光を受けて輝いて跳ねるかと思えば、おおらかにせせらぎをつくる。青い芝生と蒼い空は、広く華麗な空間を提供し、それは園遊会の舞台装置ともなる。そののびやかな空間を鬱蒼とした樹木が取り囲む。その立体感とたおやかな東山を遠くに仰ぎ見る視線は、山のあなたを空想させる。無鄰庵をつくるにあたって、山縣が望んだのはお寺の庭や町家の坪庭にみられる伝統的な侘び、寂びの世界とは違うものだった。のびやかで、明るい、自然の美しさを表現する庭であった。山縣の意向を汲みとり、その制約のなかで植治は自らの才能と技量を発揮した。山縣と植治、そして久原のこうした出会いから、近代の日本庭園が誕生した。タブーを取り払い、新たな挑戦に喝采を送る明治という時代の感性の発露をここにみることになる。

3　流れを堰き止めるように石を連ねる
「瀬落ち」が石橋の向こうに見える。
流れに変化を与えられた水は
かろやかな響きを発する
The geometrically shaped bridge contrasts with
the natural rocks in the stream

4　無鄰庵には二筋の流れがある。
右手の茶室の前を流れるのは草川の水、
奥の滝から流れ出しているのが疏水。
流れをゆったりと蛇行させることで
奥行きをみせる
Expansive sloping lawns and meandering streams,
the archetype of the modern Japanese garden

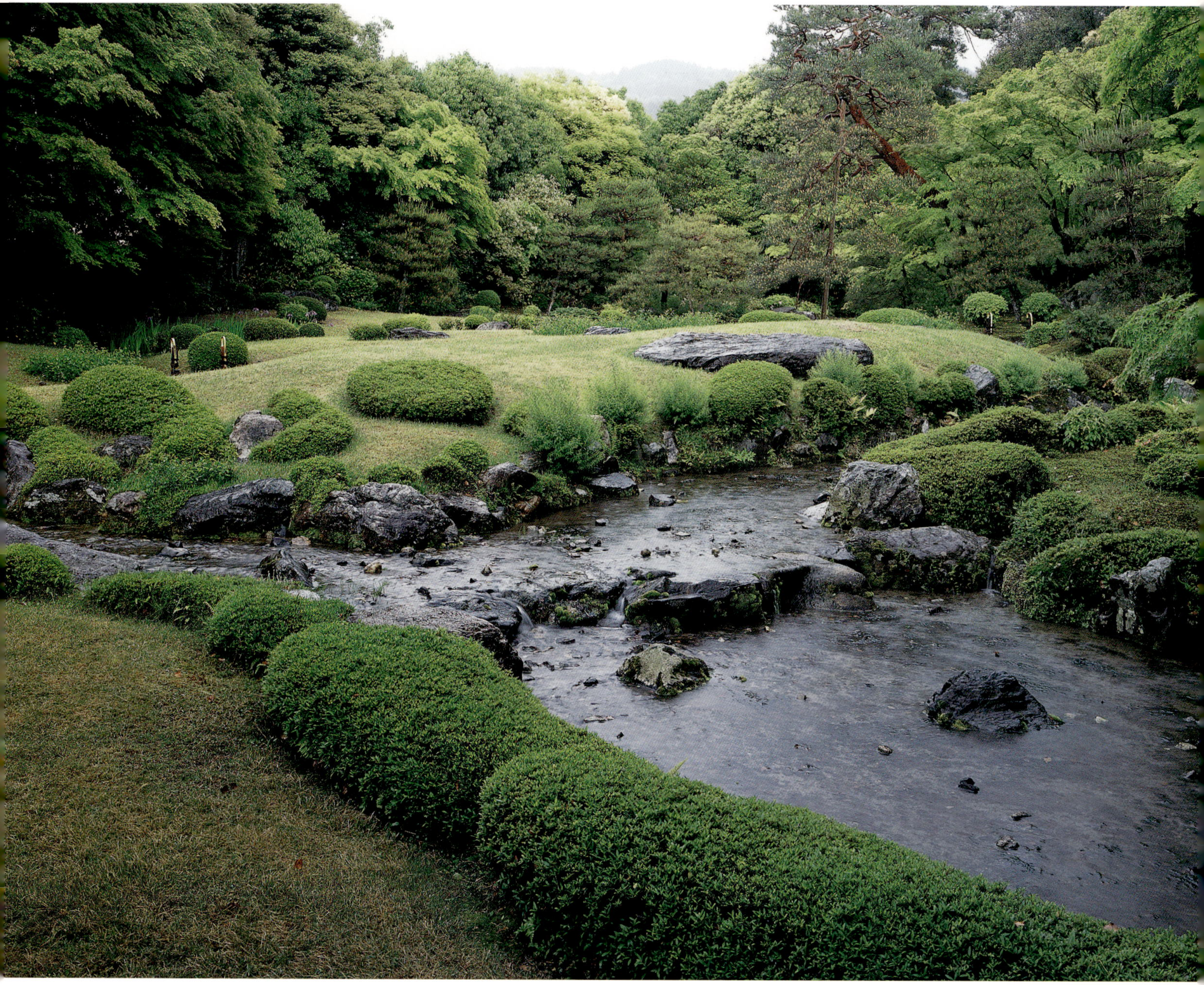

6 　川床のところどころに小石がさらりと埋め込まれている。
水の動きに変化をつける意図がある

A millstone reused as a stepping stone in the stream

5 　庭の奥の滝へと導く沢飛石。大きく弧を描いて歩くようにできている。
中央の石はそのことを隠す配置になっていて、足の置けない石が使われている

The stepping stones describe a gentle arc in the stream and lead to the waterfall

7 　「秀吉の忘れ石」の巨石は醍醐の山中から運ばれてきた。
山縣の反徳川の姿勢と結びつけられることもある

This ornamental stone emanates a strong sense of presence

8 池の岸は、平安期の庭園にみるような州浜。小石が気品のあるやわらかな曲線を描く

The pond's curved shore made of tiny rocks is reminiscent of the gardens of ancient Japanese aristocrats

Borrowing the Higashiyama hills as back ground scenery, the garden looks much larger than it is in reality. Surrounded by trees, the mounds of the lawn describe gentle curved lines and create a very bright space in the center of the garden. Within those mounds, two refreshing streams meander and murmur. Every detail was taken into account and all the effects were precisely calculated, but in the end this garden looks natural. For his villa Murin-an, YAMAGATA Aritomo did not want a traditional Kyoto garden with dense plantations and religious symbols. He wanted a modern garden with bright, open spaces that recreate natural scenic beauty. Ueji grasped YAMAGATA's intentions and within those constraints, he showed his talent. It is no exaggeration to say that the modern Japanese garden was born from their collaboration on Murin-an.

9　奥山の風情は、林を抜けると一転して平地の流れへと変貌する。
あまりに急激な展開に賛否両論がある

The water flows into the garden from a huge waterfall

10　三段の滝の流れを上からのぞく。
流れの方向をさまざまに変えながら落ちるよう計算しつくされている

The waterfall seen from above

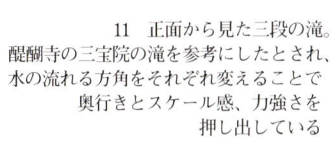

11　正面から見た三段の滝。
醍醐寺の三宝院の滝を参考にしたとされ、
水の流れる方角をそれぞれ変えることで
奥行きとスケール感、力強さを
押し出している

In contrast with the peaceful mood of the
pond, the waterfall is very powerful

12　植栽を中心とする坪庭。小さく低く抑えた石と涼やかに幹を伸ばすシホウチク（四方竹）。葉に反射したやわらかい光が室内を照らす

In NAMIKAWA's inner garden, the stone was standing. In Murin-an, the stones are lying down

14　繊細な枝ぶりの樹木に、洗練された姿に加工した手水鉢は、いかにも都市的であり、モダンでもある

A spindly washbasin on the edge of the veranda

13　手水鉢と燈篭は自然の素朴な味わいをみせる。割った竹と太い樹木が山中の草庵を想起させるが、前石には加工石を置き、人工を意識させる

An interesting hewn stone lies in front of the washbasin

施主・山縣有朋（1838-1922）
山縣有朋は、山口県萩に生まれ、吉田松陰に学び、高杉晋作らと倒幕運動に活躍。やがて西欧の軍事制度を視察し、徴兵制を取り入れる。1889年と1898年の二度にわたり内閣総理大臣の職に就き、晩年は元勲として政界に大きな影響を与えた。無鄰庵の敷地内には、主屋のほかに茶室、洋館が建てられた。1903年4月には、山縣有朋、伊藤博文、桂太郎首相、小村寿太郎外相の4人が日露戦争を決断した「無鄰庵会議」の場となった。東京には「椿山荘」、小田原に「古稀庵」、大磯に「小淘庵」の別荘を設け、庭づくりに才能を発揮した。

YAMAGATA Aritomo (1838-1922)
Born in Hagi, in Yamaguchi prefecture, he was a general in the army and created the conscription system in Japan, he was also prime minister twice, in 1889 and 1898.

The two-storied Western-style building in YAMAGATA's villa Murin-an is famous because it was here that the "Murin-an Conference" on the Japan-Russian War was held in 1903, attended by the most influential Japanese politicians at that time. YAMAGATA also worked on the construction of villas in Tokyo, Kanagawa prefecture and other areas, and showed a great interest and ability in landscape design.

15　庭の中央の瓢箪形の浅い池。浅くすることで池を広く見せる効果がある

A shallow pond looks larger than a deep one

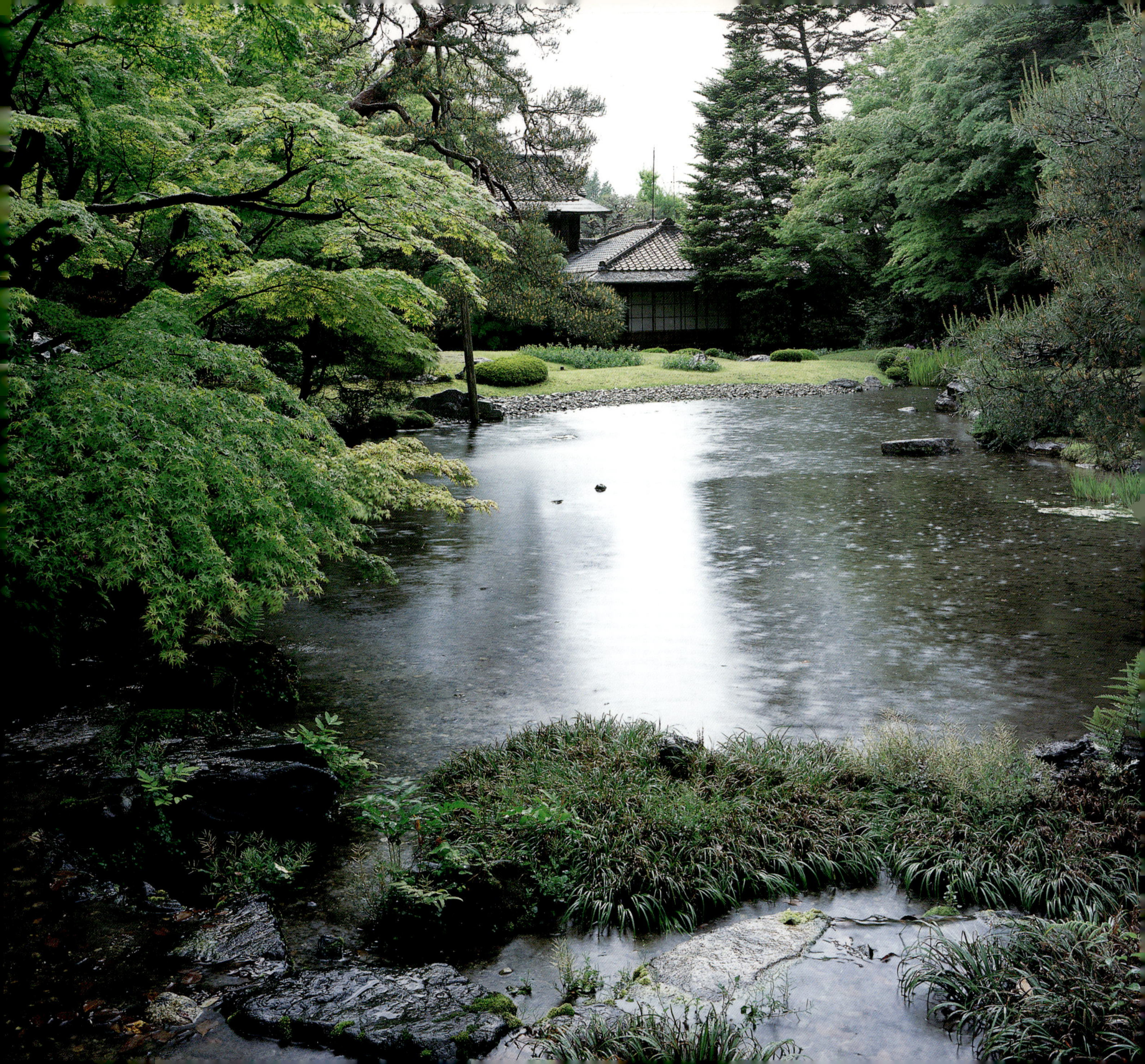

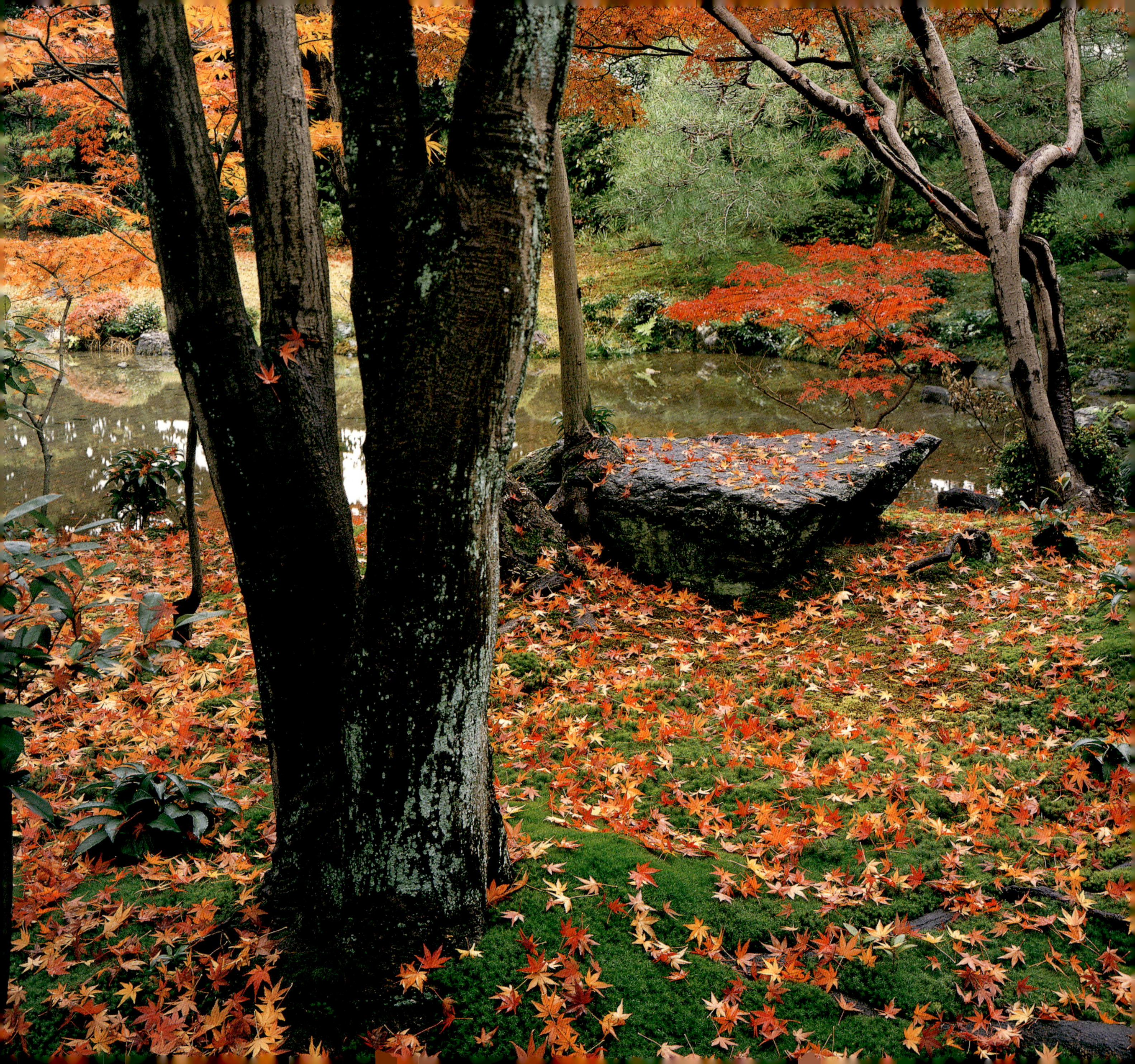

「変化」を許容する表現素材

イラストレーター、絵本作家　永田 萌

初めて無鄰庵を訪れたのは、フランスの長旅から帰ってきてすぐ。「お帰り」と出迎えられたようで心の底からホッとしました。

サラサラと音をたてて流れる水辺にそって林の奥へと進むと、豊かな水が流れる三段の滝が。まるで山奥の霧雰囲気でしょう。滝口の沢飛石の中ほどで立ち止まると、流れ落ちた水はすぐに勢いをゆるめて、私の足許をするりと抜けて流れる。その流れを追って振り返ると、こんどは秋の日射しをうけた水がキラキラと……。やさしく包み込んでくれるおおらかさに、「私はこんな場所にいたかったんだ」。

山から湧き出た水は、あと戻りすることなく先へ先へと流れ、野山を潤し、大海にそそぎ、やがて空に戻る。そのダイナミックな循環を小さな庭のなかで感じさせる力は、みごとというしかないですね。

時とともに成長し変化するのが庭。変化を許容する表現素材は、日本人の宇宙観を表現するのかも。あの日、私が受けとった光と風、せせらぎの音は、いつか私の絵のなかで表現したいですね。

◆ In the garden ...
N<small>AGATA</small> Moe
Illustrator

"The first time I visited Murin-an, it was after a long trip to France. I felt wrapped in the natural atmosphere of the garden and it was as if it were saying: "welcome back."
 Following the stream, I walked to the end of the garden and, surrounded by trees, I entered semi-darkness. In front of me, the powerful waterfall made me feel like I were very deep in the mountains. I stopped on a stepping stone in the middle of the stream and looked at the water flowing under my feet. When I looked back, the scenery had changed completely; a very calm and bright space opened in front of me.
 In a garden the plants grow and die, everything is in perpetual movement. In this way, I think that gardens, which allow for change, are a very mysterious medium for artistic expression. The sound of the stream, the light and the wind, all the feelings I experienced in Murin-an garden, I would like to express them in my illustrations one day."

16　秋の色に染められた景石
This ornamental stone is lying naturally as if it had fallen from the mountain

17　春と秋、季節のうつろいとともに表情を変える無鄰庵。
それぞれの美があり、それぞれに情緒がある
In autumn, even the stream is painted in red

平安神宮神苑

京都市左京区岡崎西天王町
1895-1913、1914-1926年作庭／33,000m²（約10,000坪）／発注者・平安遷都千百年紀年祭協賛会

1　鴨川に架かっていた
秀吉由縁の橋の石柱は、
景石としても使用されている
Ornamental stones hidden in the pond

春はシダレザクラ、初夏はカキツバタにハナショウブ、秋は紅葉、冬は雪景色と折々に趣を変えて心をなごませる神苑。心に平安の訪れがあるようにとの植治の願いが込められているのだろうか

平安神宮は1895年、平安奠都千百年記念祭にあわせて創建された。794年に都を京都に移した桓武天皇と明治天皇の父である孝明天皇を祀る。紀念祭を1年遅れで催行したのは、並行して開催する「第四回内国勧業博覧会」がシカゴ万国博の開催と重なったためだとする説が有力だが、異論もある。

内国勧業博覧会は、4月1日から7月末までの会期に京都の住民の5倍を超す113万人が入場する大イベントとなった。岡崎が会場に選ばれたのは、開発が容易な農地が拡がり、疏水の水と、その水を利用した水力発電の電力が豊富なことが理由。日本初の市街電車を同じ1895年2月に走らせた京都電気鉄道会社は、4月1日には京都駅近くから会場正面までの路線を開業させた。平安宮の大極殿を模した本殿は3月には完成し、ご祭神の桓武天皇が鎮座。

植治もまた、前年秋から構想づくりにはいり、現在の東・西・南・中の神苑のうち、白虎池を囲む西神苑と蒼龍池を核とする中神苑の一部をつくり、まにあわせた。秀吉が造営し廃材となっていた五条大橋と三条大橋の橋材・橋柱を池に渡して臥龍橋とした。

かくして、公共事業を短期間でまとめた手腕は行政など公的機関から高く評価され、植治は疏水との関わりを強めることになった。植治は、栖鳳池を中心とする東神苑を1916年に完成させ、ほぼ現在の姿とした。

Heian-jingū Garden

Heian-jingū is a Shinto shrine built in 1895, for the 1,100th anniversary of the establishment of Heian-kyō (the old name for Kyoto). The Shrine is dedicated to Emperor Kanmu, who moved the capital to Kyoto in 794, and to Emperor Kōmei, the father of Emperor Meiji.

Heian-jingū is surrounded by three ponds, to the west, the north and the east. As he did in the Namikawa Cloisonné Museum of Kyoto and in Murin-an, Ueji drew water from the Lake Biwa Canal. He also used the canal also to bring large quantities of rocks from Moriyama, on the west cost of the lake Biwa. He managed to get hold of the discarded pillars of the former Sanjō and Gojō bridges in Kyoto and used them to create very original stepping stones crossing the pond.

The garden was constructed in three stages. In 1895, Ueji first created the West and Middle Gardens. In 1897, he made the stream linking those two ponds. Then in 1916, on the east side of the shrine, he created the East Garden.

2 三条大橋と五条大橋の橋桁と橋脚の石柱を使った臥龍橋は、中神苑のビューポイントであり親水空間。石は、しだいに小さく、丸くなってジグザグに。自分の足で渡るのも楽しい

Reusing the discarded pillars from ancient bridges in Kyoto, Ueji created these stepping stones that snake across the pond

3 西神苑へと落ちる滝は、
流れをつくって白虎池へとつづく。
滝石組や遣り水の技巧にも注目したい。

This waterfall gives rythm to the stream
between the West and the Middle Garden

4 せせらぎを渡す沢飛石。
沢渡りともよばれ、
水の流れの変化を楽しませる。
奥の石は、橋添石*とも
橋鋏み石ともいい、
高さを違えて景趣をつくる

Stepping stones crossing the stream

平安神宮と平安奠都千百年紀念祭 明治維新とともに天皇が車駕東幸されると、公家をはじめ出入りの業者に至るまでが京都を出る事態になった。人口は、江戸期の40万前後から1871年（明治4）には23万7,000にまで激減する。幕末の戦乱の影響もあったとはいえ、京都は疲弊していた。明治政府は京都市民へのお詫びの意味を込めて10万両の下賜金と15万両の貸付金を下付した。この資金をもとに、京都は産業の振興と再生をはかった。明石博高が主導して1870年に設立した舎密局は、その代表格。石鹸、ラムネ、麦酒、ガラス、陶磁器のほか、並河靖之が成功を収めた七宝焼の釉薬を開発する。そして、琵琶湖疏水の建設と奠都千百年を紀念して「第四回内国勧業博覧会」を招致する。そのパビリオンの一つとして計画したのが、8分の5サイズに縮小した太極殿。建築を担当した一人が、のちに文化勲章を受章する伊東忠太。当時、25歳であった。これに並行して、「平安奠都千百年祭紀念殿」を、奠都を実行した桓武天皇を祀る平安神宮とする計画がもち上がった。紀念祭は1年遅れて10月22日から24日まで行なわれた。このときの時代行列を祭礼化したのが現在の時代祭。

The 1,100th anniversary of the establishment of Heian-kyō (the old name for Kyoto)

Just after the Meiji Restoration, the Emperor moved to the new capital, Tokyo, and Kyoto fell into decline. But Kyoto soon started to promote industry and in 1895, the 4th Industrial Exposition of Japan was held together with the 1,100th anniversary of the establishment of Heian-kyō (the old name for Kyoto). Heian-jingū shrine was built for this occasion. The procession held for that event is the origin of the "Festival of the Ages," one of the three most important festivals in Kyoto.

山縣有朋と久原庄三郎の二人の指示、なかでも洋風の教養と庭について深い見識をそなえた山縣に従いつつ無鄰庵を作庭していた植治のもとに、平安神宮の神苑を作庭する話が飛び込んできた。依頼してきたのは中井弘知事。薩摩の出身でやはり元は維新の志士。

　因襲的な作風がありがたがられる江戸の中・末期以降の様式を打破し、奔放に空間をデザインすることのおもしろさを山縣に学んだ植治は、短い期間に空間をデザインする能力を身につけていた。それは、意味ありげにみせる象徴空間の庭を、のびやかな自然主義へと回帰させるものだった。

　植治は平安神宮の神苑で、その力をぞんぶんに発揮した。神の存在を思わせる深淵で厳格な雰囲気の庭でなく、桜の花吹雪が舞い散り、柳の新芽が風にたなびき、池の水が鏡のように蒼空や緑の樹木を明るく映しだす世界。晴れやかで、風が薫る、広々とした神苑に、人びとはゆったりと散策しながら自然にふれる。さまざま生命の尊い息吹を感じつつ、人びとは生きていることの喜びを実感する。

　谷崎潤一郎の『細雪』や川端康成の『古都』で描写されたこの空間は、明治の人びとに明るい未来を予感させる鮮烈な印象を与えた。

As KAWABATA Yasunari wrote in his famous novel "Old Capital," nobody can stay indifferent in front of the graceful beauty of the garden of Heian-jingū shrine.

While Ueji was working on the Murin-an garden with YAMAGATA Aritomo, he was requested by the Governor of Kyoto prefecture to create the garden for Heian-jingū. It was Ueji's first large-scale project and even today it is one of the most visited gardens in Kyoto.

Instead of a mystic garden with very dense plantations as in traditional Shinto shrines, he created very refined and luminous spaces, where many flowers come into blossom all year long. Without the water from the Lake Biwa Canal, Ueji would have never been able to create the three large ponds he did. At that time, it was revolutionary in its conception.

In Heian-jingū, Ueji demonstrated the skills he had polished with YAMAGATA Aritomo and established his reputation as a creator of modern Japanese gardens.

5　大小の石を、
さまざまな向きにおくことで
力強い自在な流れを表現している。
護岸石組の扱いは、
庭の景観に大きな違いを与える

Ueji raised the stones to strengthen the stream banks

6　石の配置の妙を楽しめる流れが
東神苑へとつづく。
流れの石組は流水に変化を与える。

Even though it's man-made, this stream looks more than natural

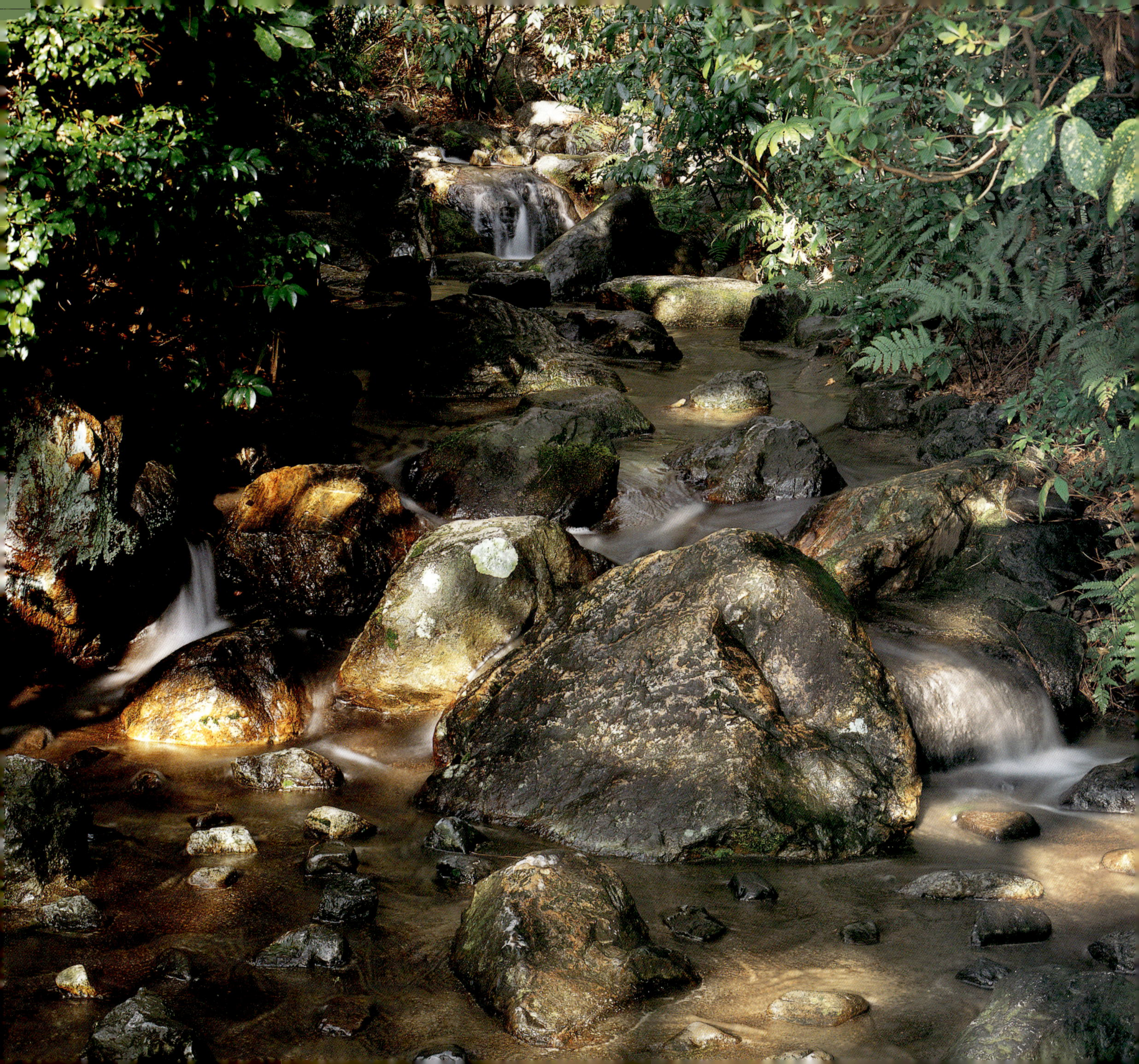

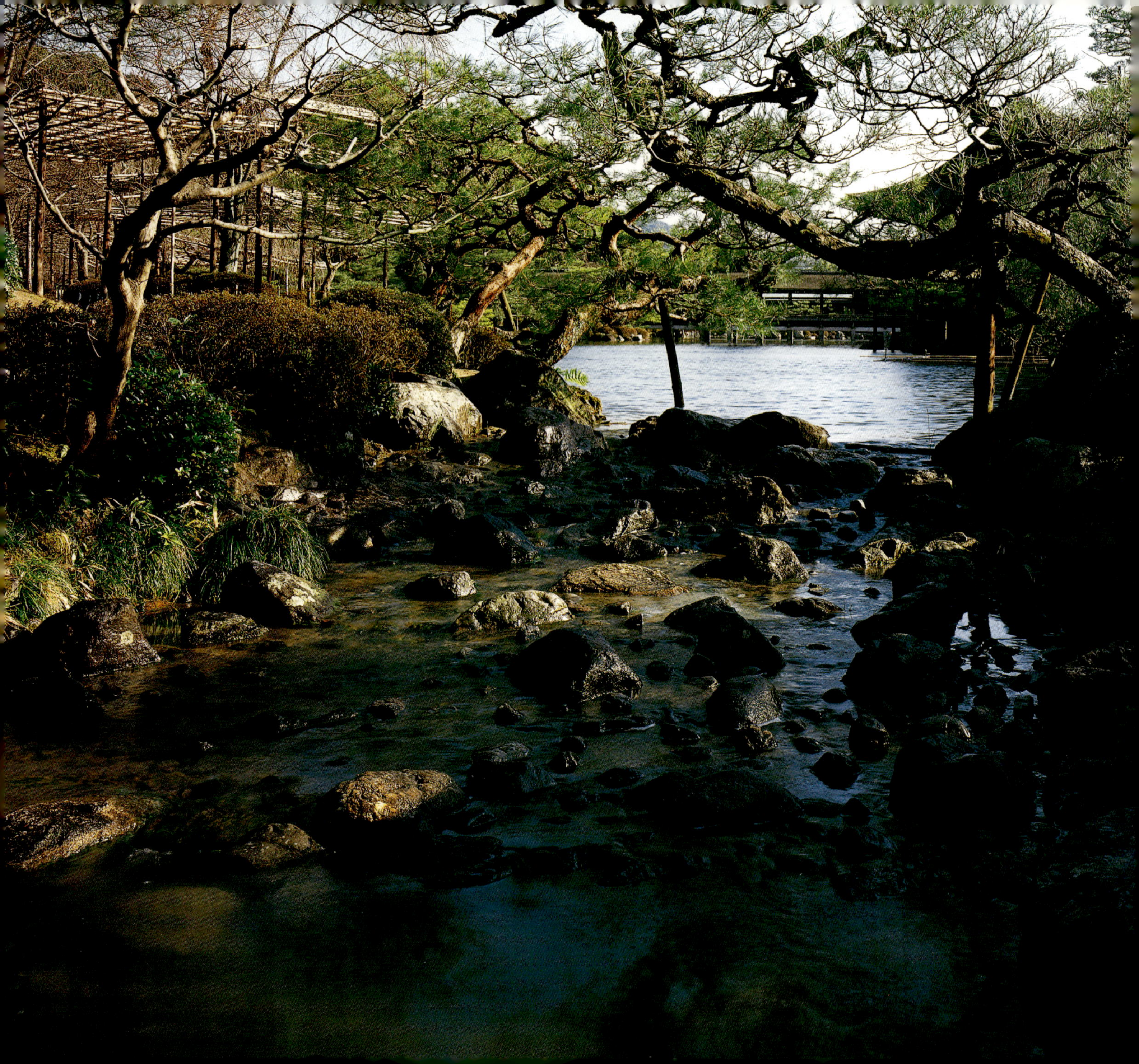

7 東神苑の水は中神苑に流れ、やがて西神苑へと流れる。神苑は穏やかで静の空間だが、神苑と神苑とをつなぐ流れは、いずれもやや野性的で、動の空間であることを意識させる
The overflow of the East Pond

8 東神苑に浮かぶ中島。鶴島、亀島、蓬莱山などを象徴するものではないところに植治らしさがある
The two islands in the East pond

植治の庭はビオトープ

森本幸裕　京都大学大学院地球環境学堂教授

京都の庭を眺めるとき、その庭をとりまく環境にまで視野を拡げてほしい。とくに植治さんの庭を語るとき、この視点ははずせません。

庭は人為的につくられた自然ですが、剪定や池さらいなど、人の手がときどきはいることによって、自然のプロセスが促進される面があります。木々を剪定すると、たくさんの光が地面に射し込みますから、苔や低木は育ちます。

平安神宮の神苑には、三つの池とそれをつなぐ流れがあります。琵琶湖疏水の水を引き込んでつくられた池です。形状の異なる苑路を歩きながら、池の岸辺や池と池とを結ぶ流れをよく観察してください。流れが早いところと遅いところ、光がふりそそいできらきらと輝く浅瀬があったり、枝が生い茂って薄暗く、深い淵のような場所があったりと、水の景はじつに多様です。ショウブや水草など、水辺の植物の種類も豊富です。

疏水を通って運ばれてきたのは水だけではありません。琵琶湖からさまざまな魚介類もやってきて、この平安神宮をはじめ、疏水の水を引き込んでいる岡崎一帯の庭の池で成長しています。興味深いのは、琵琶湖ではすでに絶滅の危機にあるイチモンジタナゴが、この神苑の池で世代交代までしていること。この池には、卵を産み、稚魚が育つ環境が整っていることを意味します。

平安神宮の神苑を歩くと、なつかしい気分になる人も多いんじゃないでしょうか。豊かな生命が息づいているからです。植治さんの100年前の庭はいま、絶滅危惧種のレフュージア（避難場所）としての機能も果たしているのです。

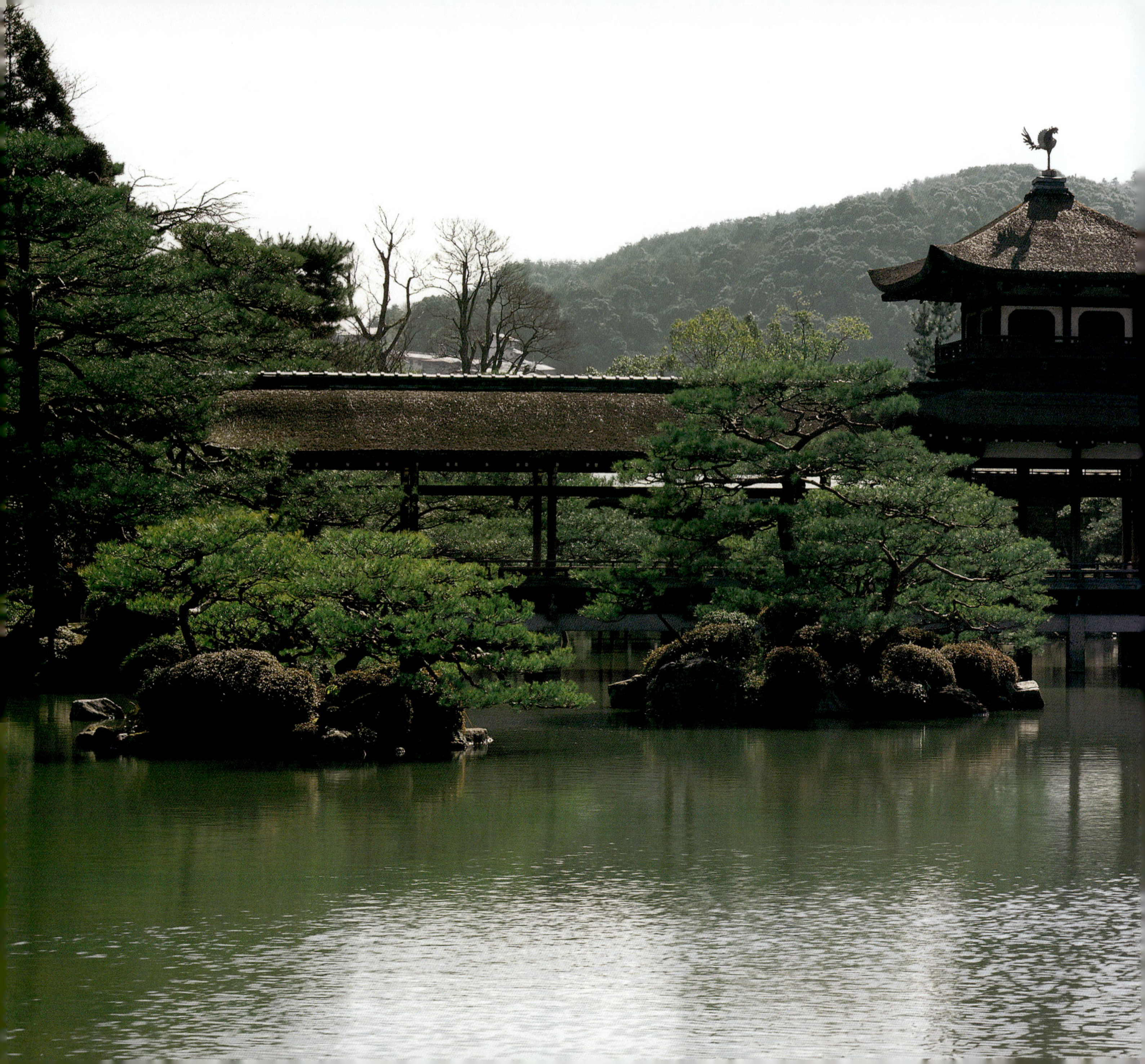

◆ **In the garden ...**
MORIMOTO Yukihiro
Professor at the University of Kyoto

"It's important to think about gardens as complete environments. And this, goes especially for the gardens created by Ueji.
 Like all the gardens by Ueji in this area, the water for Heian-jingū has been drawn from the Lake Biwa Canal. After investigation, we realized that not only water but also lots of fish came along the canal and are now living in those ponds. Even more interesting is that fish like the Acheilognathus cyanostigma, which are in danger of extinction in Lake Biwa took refuge here. This means that the necessary environment for those fish to live and lay eggs is present in the ponds created by Ueji.
 One hundred years ago, one of the purposes of those ponds was to protect the shrine from the fire; now they are working as a refuge for species in danger of extintion."

9 東神苑に架かる泰平閣（橋殿）は、植治の作庭にあわせて大正時代に京都御所から移築。通路の両側では腰をかけて眺めを楽しんだり、涼んだりできる。木造寄棟重層造り総桧皮葺

This bridge was brought from the imperial palace in 1916

何有荘庭園 (旧和楽庵)

京都市左京区南禅寺福地町46
1905-09年作庭（1917、22、28年改修）/約20,000m²（約6,000坪）/施主・稲畑勝太郎

錦鯉が泳ぎ、錦秋の東山を
映す池の周辺には
正装した人たちが集い、
グラスをあわせる。
賓客を迎えての煌びやかな
明治のガーデン・パーティは、
あたかも昨日のできごと
だったかのよう……

1　草堂に至る小径から見下ろした数寄屋の主屋と洋館。眺望は黒谷と吉田山
General view of the Kaiu-sō villa

明治政府の神仏分離策で南禅寺が手放した塔頭跡を稲畑勝太郎が手に入れた1905年に、作庭工事ははじまっている。

8年ものフランス留学で西欧の科学・技術を学び、のちに大阪商工会議所会頭や貴族院議員まで務めることになる稲畑は、広大な庭に平屋の和風住宅と欧風の建築、それに茶室などをもうけて「和楽庵」と名付け、自宅とした。

傾斜地を登って草葺きの茶室「草堂」に向かう途中にはトンネルを掘った。トンネルは二つに分かれ、一つは草堂の地階に導き、一つは南を流れる疏水べりへと誘う。第一次世界大戦を経験した稲畑は、これからの時代は自ら身を守る設備が必要だと実感したという。

大正から戦後にかけての和楽庵には、政財界の巨頭や取引先の接待のほか、国際人稲畑らしく海外の元首、高官、賓客が頻繁に訪れた。海外から京都を訪れた人たちにも、日本理解に役だつと開放した。

稲畑の死後、1953年にこれを譲り受けた大宮庫吉は、「何か有るようで何も無い、何も無いようで何かが有る」という禅語にちなんで「何有荘」と改名した。

2006年から大がかりな修復を進め、掲載したのは、ようやく落ち着きをみせた2007年秋の写真。

Kaiu-sō Garden

Kaiu-sō was the former villa of INABATA Katsutarō, a rich businessman of the Meiji period. At the time, it was called "Waraku-an" but it was renamed "Kaiu-sō" post-war.

INABATA bought this former annex of Nanzen-ji temple in 1905. There is still a belfry in a corner of the garden, the last vestige of the temple.

The garden was created over a long period. Ueji did the first construction in 1905 and remodeled it several times up to 1928. Drawing water from the Lake Biwa Canal that flows just behind the site, Ueji created three streams that meander down the slope to a pond in front of the villa. This garden can be appreciated from inside the Japanese-style reception room or by walking along the path leading to the top of the hill.

There are two tearooms and two waiting rooms for the traditional tea ceremony but INABATA, who had studied for eight years in France, also used his villa to organize garden parties with Japanese high-society and his foreign guests.

2 茶を楽しむあいだも、せせらぎが和音を奏でる。残月亭は、植治の想う「市中の山居」

The thatch roofed waiting room enclosed by a stream

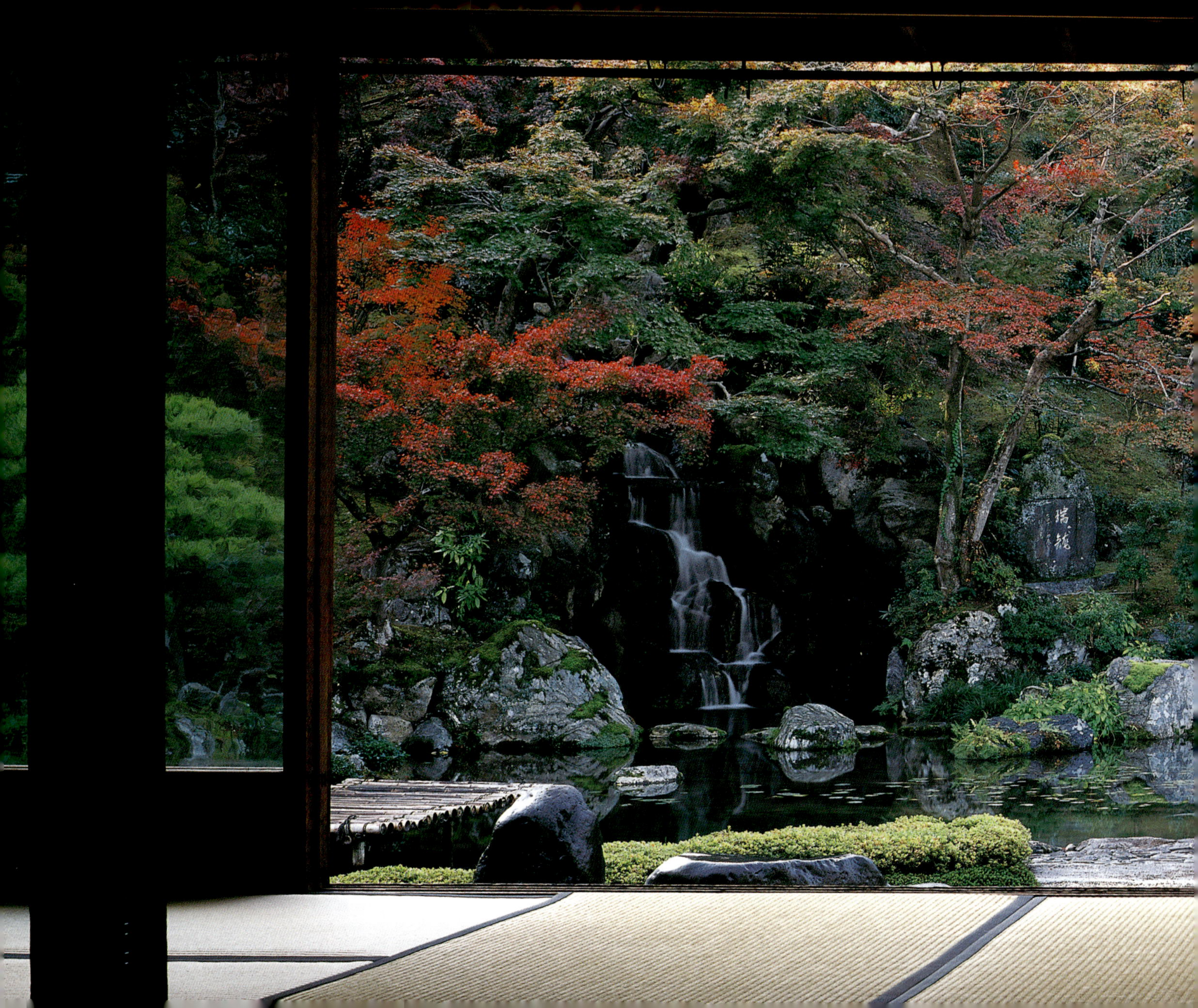

3　座敷から南庭を眺める。瑞龍滝は、座敷の正面にてではなく、はすかいに落ちるよう構成されたことで品よく収まる。右手の鐘楼は、この地がかつて南禅寺の塔頭であった名残
The main waterfall is not facing the reception room but was set off to the side

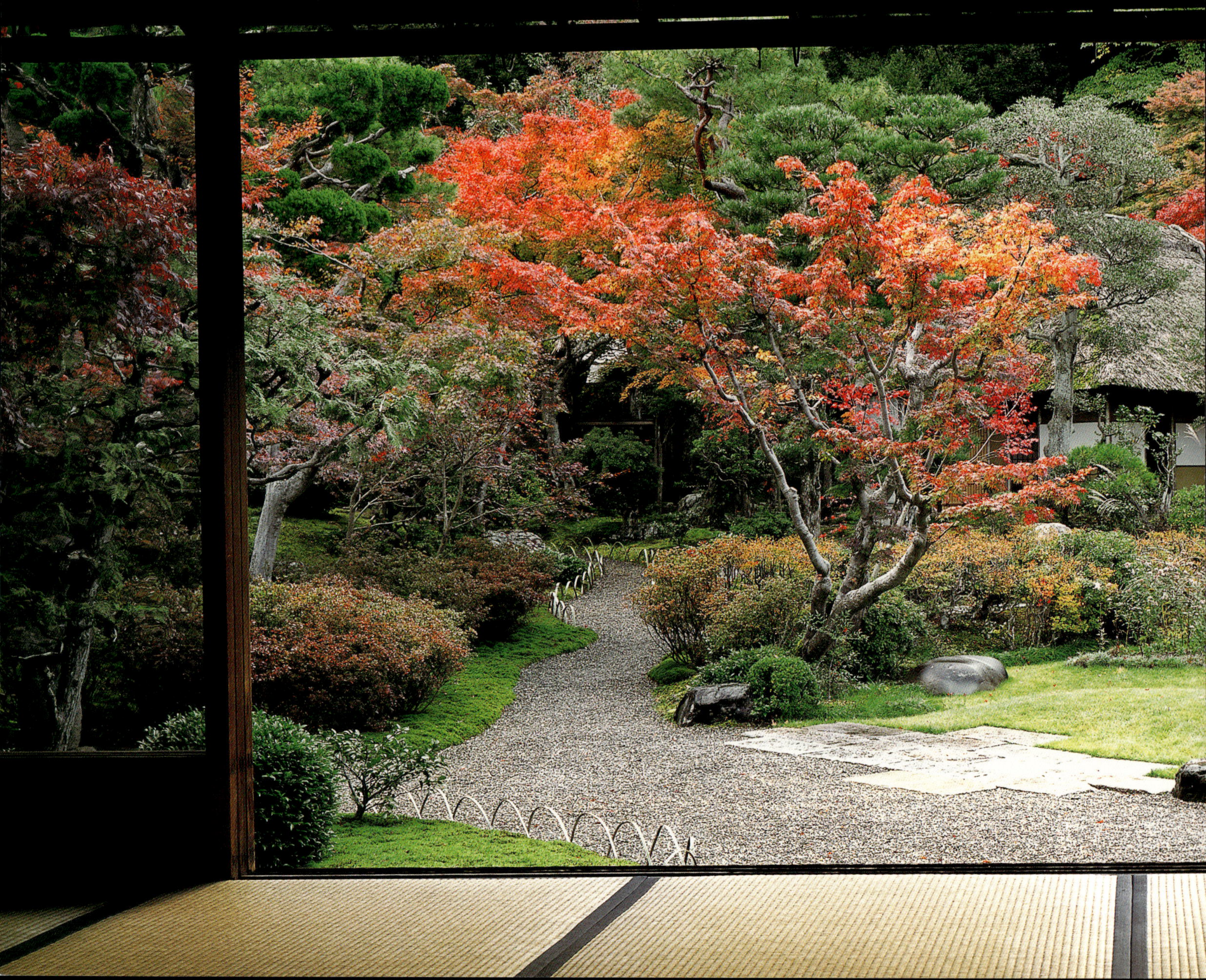

4　座敷から東庭を眺める。左手の道はゆったりと山に誘う。木立に見え隠れするのは浅目亭
The view of the thatch roofed and the Higashiyama hills gives this garden a very rural feeling

無鄰庵同様に、数寄屋建築と洋館、それに茶室を組み合わせ、その前面に芝生と池が拡がる構成はいかにも明治という時代を感じさせる。

座敷から眺める雄大な滝は、白い飛沫をあげながら岩肌を走り落ちる。東山から伝い落ちてきたかのように思わせる水も、じつは疏水の水。このあたりでは、東山の中腹の高い所を流れている。

座敷から見ると聳え立つ斜面は野性の自然と閉塞感を感じさせるが、不思議と坂を登る苦痛を感じないのは計算しつくされた配置の故だろう。坂道の途中の山膚に大きくぽっかりと口を開けたトンネルを歩き、階段を登るといつのまにか草堂の中に佇んでいる趣向。

座敷は、西に鴨川、御苑、黒谷を見下ろす開放的な展望空間。ずいぶん高くまで登ったものだと思うが、その草堂の裏が疏水の分岐点であることに気づく。分線は南禅寺の水路閣へと続き、本線は蹴上の浄水場に。植治の「庭園に定まった好みなどないのは、一に地形によるからでございます」の言葉を実感する。

5 瑞龍滝。植治の滝には三段の「糸落ち」形式が多いが、この瑞龍滝は「伝い落ち」。人工の滝とはとても思えない端正な品の良さがにじみ出る
The powerful waterfall ends in a quiet pond

Kaiu-sō garden was constructed on the north slope of a hill facing the villa. On this abrupt slope, Ueji created three streams. The main stream falls almost straight down over a waterfall into a pond, just in front of the villa. Unusually in Ueji's works, this waterfall is not threadlike but slides powerfully over the rocks.

On the east side, surrounded by trees, another stream meanders down to a little pond in front of the Ryūgin-an tea pavilion. Following the stream, a path climbs to the top of the hill.

On the way up, there is a tunnel that leads directly into the second Sōdō tea pavilion. After World War I, it seems that INABATA felt the need to create a safe refuge in his garden to protect himself and his relatives. However, it's interesting to note the presence of a crouching basin for washing hands and mouth before tea ceremony. It means that this tunnel could also work like a traditional tea garden path.

6 滝壺のそばにかかる沢飛石。存在感を抑えて抑えて表現する植治らしい技巧。滝に落ちた水は静かに拡がり、水平と垂直の調和をつくる

Stepping stones crossing the pond just in front of the waterfall

7　1895年の第四回内国博覧会に出品された茶室、龍吟庵が移築されている
Stepping stones leading to the Ryūgin-an tearoom

8　自然石を基本に敷き詰めて奥へ奥へとたゆたう園路をドウダンツツジが飾る。平面と曲面の調和は、植治の見つけた「人工を自然たらしめる法則」の一つかもしれない
The path snakes through Japanese "enkianthus" azaleas

9　残月亭のそばの流れ蹲踞。サイフォンの原理を利用して水穴の底から水を噴き上げるようにしたのが流れ蹲踞
A washbasin set in the stream

10　一文字手水鉢。右端から水がしたたり落ちるようにした構成が細長い形をさらに強調する
A washbasin made with a long hollowed-out stone

施主・稲畑勝太郎（1862-1949）
京都の和菓子の老舗「亀屋正重」の家に生まれるが、成績が優秀なことから16歳で京都府の留学生として染色技術を学ぶことを目的にフランスに。8年あまりをかけてリヨン工業学校やリヨン大学で染色理論と応用化学を修得し、染工場で徒弟として実技も学ぶ。1885年の帰国後は京都染工講習所開設に尽力。やがて現在の稲畑産業を設立し、合成染料や医薬品の輸入をはじめ、1897年には本店を大阪に移す。大学の同級生であったフランスのリュミエール兄弟が1895年に発明した撮影と映写のできる2台のシネマトグラフを技師同道で輸入、日本で初めて映画を公開上映する。稲畑は、「欧米文化ノ実況ヲ我国ニ知ラシムルニ最モ適当ナリ」と記す。

INABATA Katsutarō (1862-1949)
Born in Kyoto, he was a brilliant student and was sent to France to study muslin weaving and the latest techniques in synthetic dyeing. On his return to Japan, he established himself as a successful businessman and Inabata & Co. is today a multinational company. INABATA is also well known as one of the pioneers of Japanese cinema. In France, he made the acquaintance of Auguste Lumiere and he brought back a cinematograph. In 1897, INABATA gave Japan its first projected film.

11　龍吟庵の茶室近くの龍吟滝。東山の中腹から引き込まれた疏水は、いくつもの筋をつくって山膚を流れ落ちる
This gentle waterfall falls into the pond just in front of the Ryugin-an tearoom

12　せせらぎに架かる石橋の両脇には伝統にしたがって高さの違う橋添石が置かれ、景趣をつくっている
The path crosses the stream and meanders to the top of the hill

13　トンネル内には、手水鉢などを一段低く置いた「降り蹲踞」を据えている。湧き水を汲むイメージであろうか。
難を逃れてここで過ごすときの必需の施設でもあった
Inside the tunnel a crouching basin was created for tea ceremony

14　庭の頂上部には京都を眺望する絶景の茶室、草堂が
しつらえてある。
この草堂の地下に至るトンネルが山の中腹にもうけられ、
入口にはPestera Haiducului Carolの文字が彫られている。
Carolは1920年にここを訪れたルーマニアの皇太子の名

At the entrance of the tunnel is inscribed the name of a cave in Romania: "Pestera Haiducului" and the name of the Romanian Prince who visited Kaiu-sō, "Carol"

円山公園

京都市東山区円山町473
1913-1914年作庭／86,641m²（約26,000坪）／発注者・京都府

西洋の文物や思想を積極的に取り込む明治の日本。
都市づくりにも、パブリック・スペースとしての公園の概念が導入される。
西洋思想にもとづく公園を和の巧みと感性で飾ることを植治は考える

明治政府の神仏分離策でとり壊された祇園感神院（八坂神社）の坊舎跡や円山安養寺などの境内を官有地とし、京都府は円山公園と命名した。琵琶湖疏水を設計・監督した田辺朔郎は、疏水の水を利用する公園整備計画を立案、1893年に噴水を完成させる。田辺は、植治と同じ世代で一つ年下。それから10年後、1年をかけて拡張・整備工事がはじまった。建築家の武田五一が指揮し、造園は平安神宮の神苑で公的機関の信頼を獲得した植治が担当した。植治は、1911年に完成した第二疏水の豊かな水を利用して、滝にはじまり池に至る渓谷を自然そのままに再現した。

その植治の庭の借景となる東山の山腹を飾っていたのは、明石博高が健康増進を目的に金閣を模して設けた吉水温泉や、安養寺の塔頭（六阿弥）の一つを壊して建設された巨大洋風ホテルだった。公園内には、明治の「煙草王」と称された村井吉兵衛が贅を尽くした洋館の別邸「長楽館」が建つほか、歴史的に飲食店などが並ぶ参道であったことから、いまも風雅な佇まいの料理店や宿泊施設などが並び、珍しい景観をつくる。

Maruyama Park

Maruyama Park was the first Public Park in Kyoto. It was dedicated in 1886, on the former site of a temple at the foot of the Higashiyama hills. It was named Maruyama Park after the ancient temple, Maruyama Anyō-ji.

In 1893, with water from the Lake Biwa Canal, the first fountain in Kyoto was created in the pond. This area has been particularly famous for its cherry blossoms since the end of Edo period and today it's still one of the most frequented areas of Kyoto in spring.

Ueji worked on the Maruyama Park from 1913 to 1914. On the gentle slope of the Higashiyama hills, he created a stream that flows down to the pond.

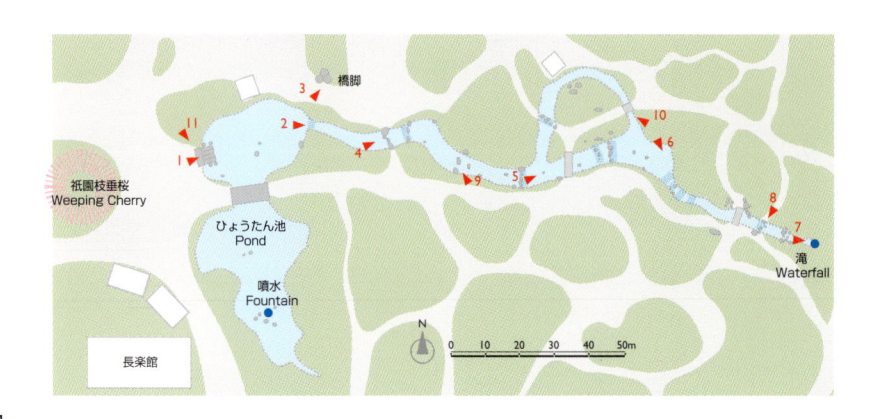

1　知恩院の華頂山から流れ出た水が、海に見立てた
　　この池に流れ込むまでを植治は描いた。
　　船着きを起点に川を遡行するにつれ
　　景観は変貌し、やがて滝に至る
　　View of the Higashiyama hills from the pond

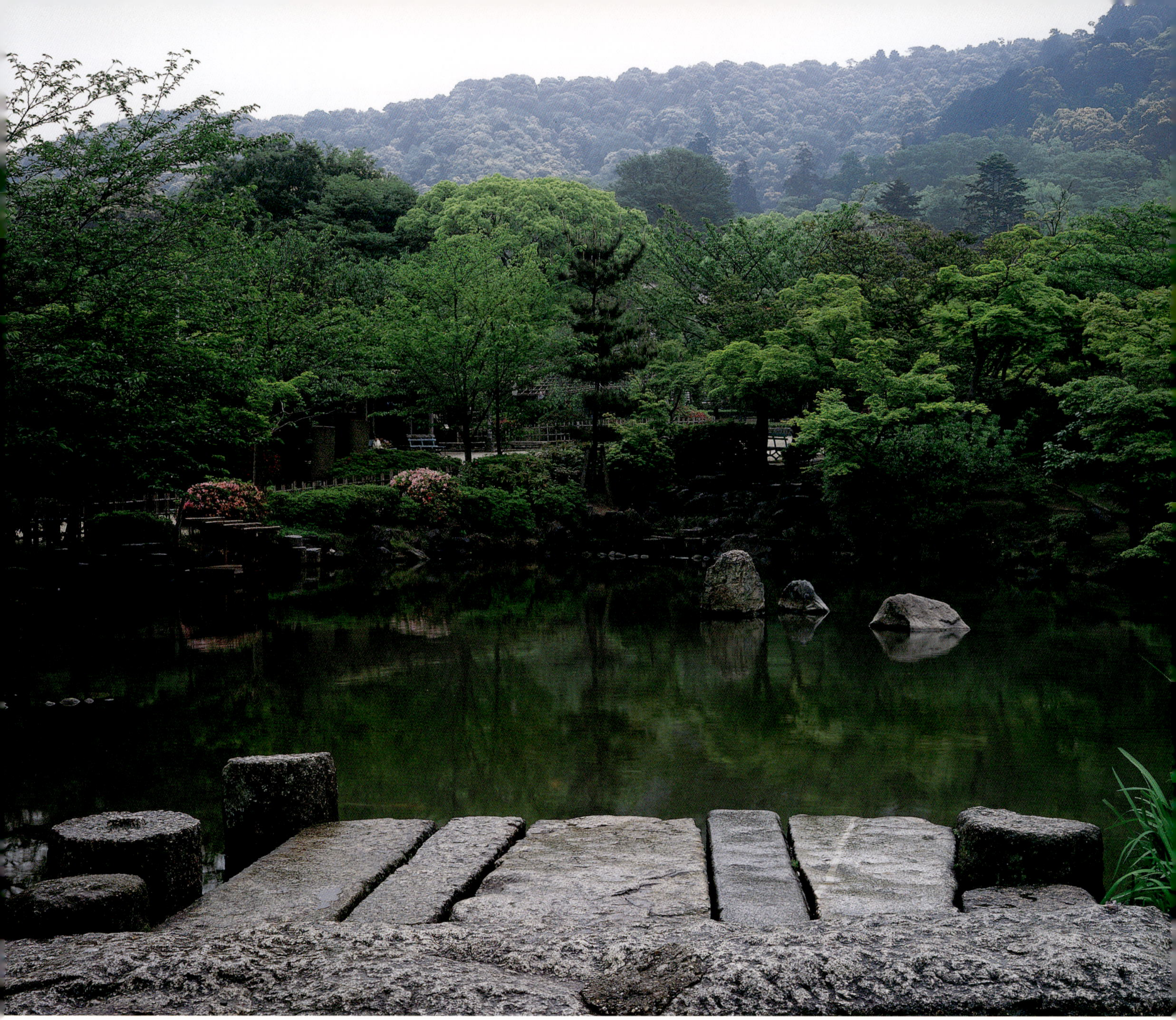

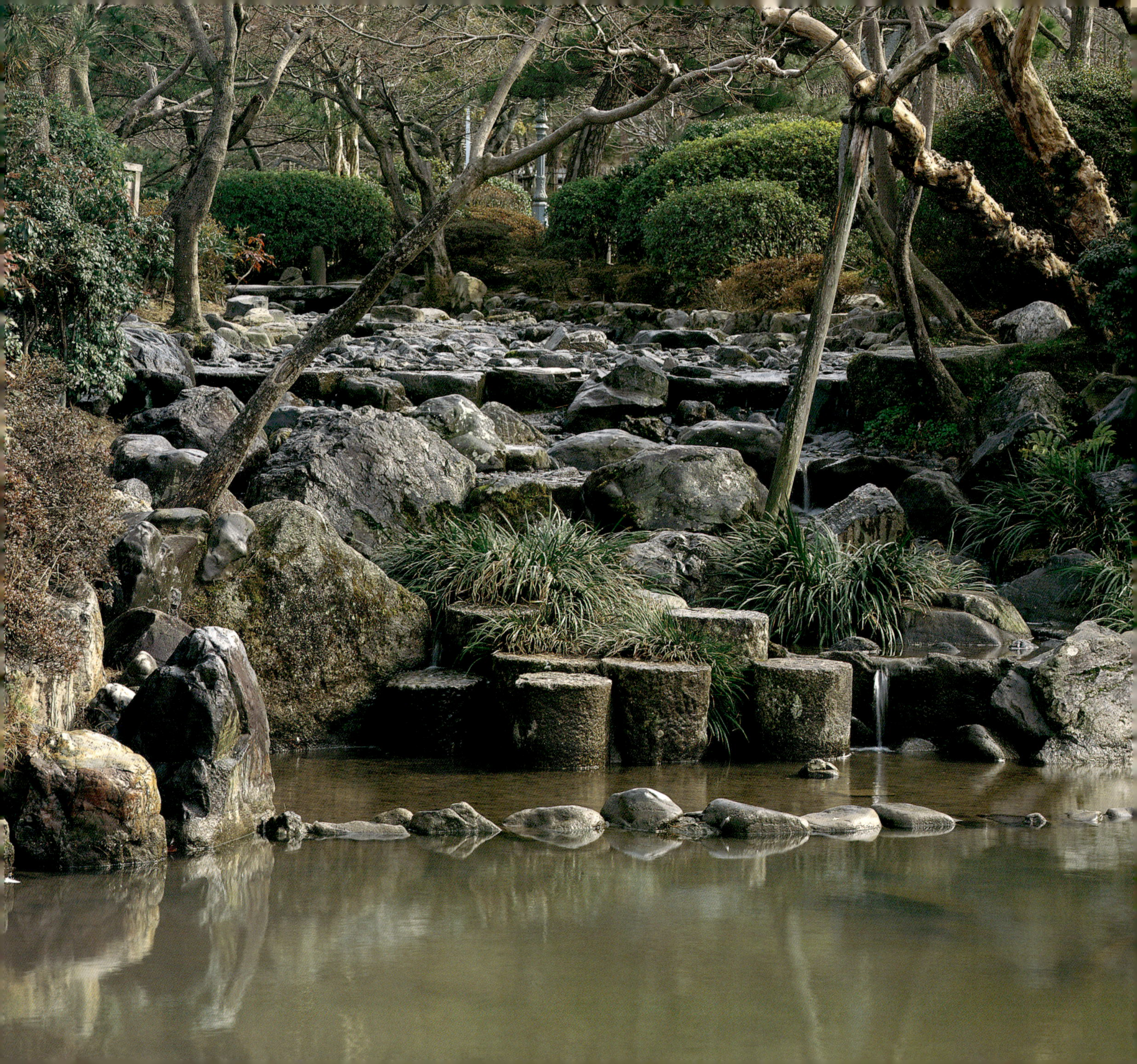

円山公園は京都で最初の公園。植治にしても、公園がなんたるものか、その概念をどこまで理解できていたかはわからない。それでも植治は、博覧会の目玉の一つとして平安神宮の神苑をつくったことで、個人の所有物ではない庭園の姿をイメージできるようになっていたのではないか。公共施設に関わることで、植治はそれまでの伝統的な植木屋から、近代造園業への転換をはかることになった。

とはいえ、植治のめざすのは、洋風の公園を真似ることではなく、あくまでも京都の伝統にもとづいた、着物のよく似あう庭づくりだった。植治は、公園に和風の庭園デザインを取り入れた。東山の山裾に、上流の滝から瓢箪形の池に至る軽快な流れを疏水の水でつくった。日本の近代造園の基本理念と様式を生み出した最初の人は、やはり植治ではなかったか。

2　流れ落ちた水はようやく穏やかな池に。何層にも積み重なる水平の層と奥行きのある高低差がのびやかな遠近感をつくる
The end of the long stream flows smoothly down into the pond

3　円山公園の桜。植治にしては珍しく景石に加工した石を使う
Maruyama Park is also very famous for its cherry blossoms

The notion of the Public Garden was introduced from Europe, and was still very new for the Japanese of the beginning of the 20th century. In Maruyama Park, Ueji did not try to copy the style of European parks but designed instead a park that fitted Japanese taste and habits.

Drawing water from the Lake Biwa Canal, he created a very natural stream, meandering down to a gourd-shaped pond. Walking in Maruyama Park is like walking along a river on a mountain path.

きき上手な植治はん

佐野藤右衛門
「植藤造園」16代目当主。円山公園の桜守

七代目植治はんとは、私の祖父の代からのつきあいです。

円山公園はゆるやかな傾斜地で、奥の滝口から落ちた水は、しぜんと低いところに流れます。元の地形や石、樹木をうまく活かすという植治はんの庭づくりの特徴は、円山公園にもよくあらわれています。植栽も、枝ぶりをつくりこんだ松よりも、癖のない木を好まはったそうです。値段の高い資材は使わず、奇抜なこともしはりません。そやけど、思わず目のとまる場所に、「きき」があるんやな。技巧がさりげなく溶けこんでいる。植治はんの庭はどれもやわらかく、おおらかな印象やけど、そのなかに緻密に計算された繊細な線がピッと走る。まるで着物の柄のようや。

植治はんはプロデューサーで、現場で手を動かすのは職人。職人の能力を組みあわせて自分のイメージを具象化する力がありますな。植治のもとで腕をみがいた人たちが京都の庭づくりに与えた影響も大きいですよ。お茶屋の露地の飛び石や町家の坪庭など、いまもあちこちに「植治流」が息づいています。

私は、この公園のシダレザクラの「桜守」とよばれてますが、初代は1948年に枯れて、いまあるのは私が植えた二代目です。

6 意図して野性の自然をつくる技術と、
　表現力のはてしない豊かさに
　驚嘆せずにはおれない
A steep slope creates rhythm in the stream

4 沢飛石と植栽が、平地に近い
　豊かな土地であることを示す
Shaped stones make a path through
this natural stream

5 橋が人里であることを示すが、
　角張った石と歪んだ松の木が
　厳しい自然のもとにあることを
　想像させる
Little rocks placed at random create
a very natural looking stream

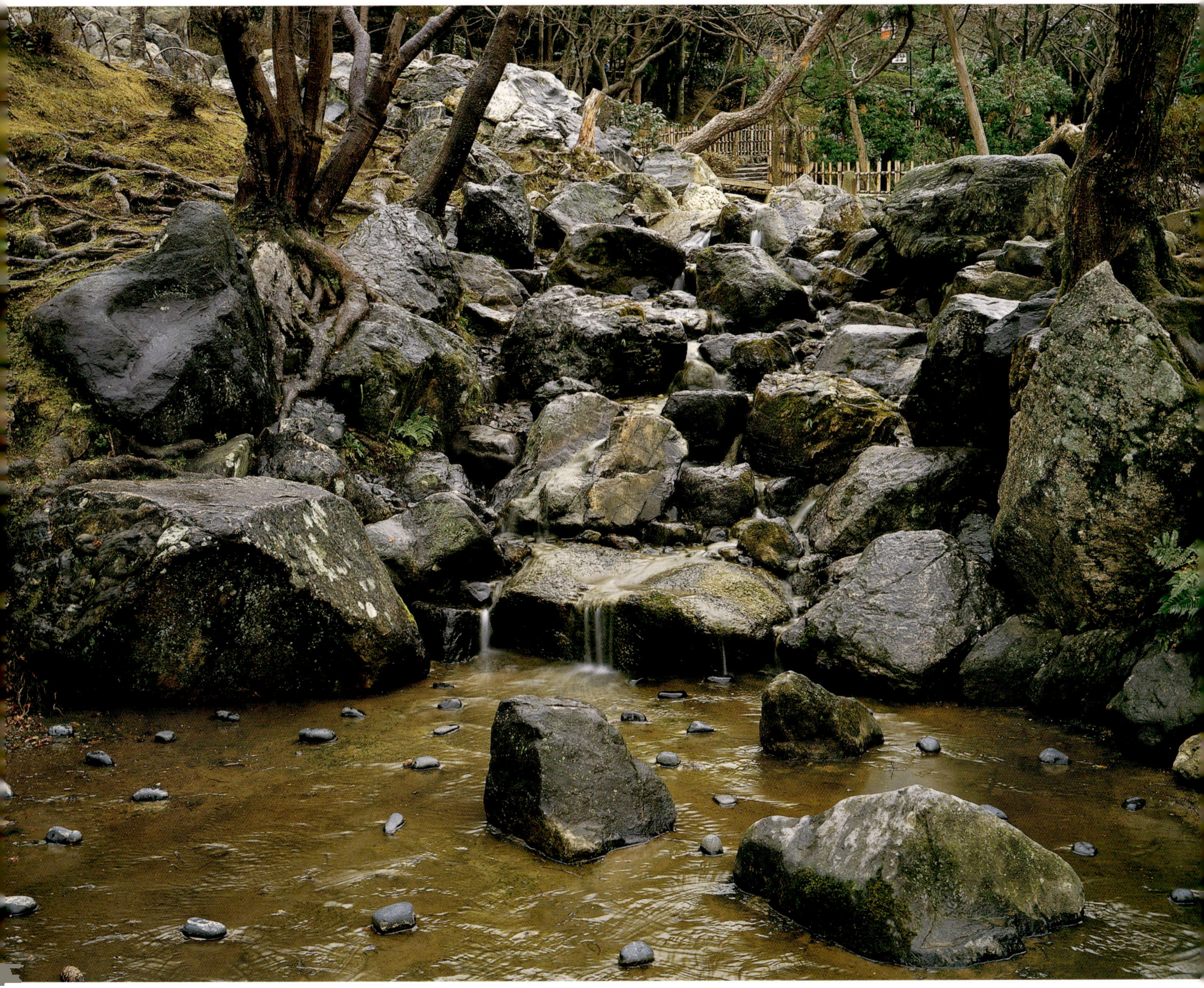

◆ **In the garden ...**
SANO Tōemon
Landscape gardener

"Mr. Ueji was an acquaintance of my father and I met him once or twice when I was a child.

The characteristic of gardens created by Mr. Ueji, that is to say, the wise use of the original topography, is especially clear in Maruyama Park. It is located at the bottom of the Higashiyama hills. From the waterfall down to the pond, the water meanders, as it would from a natural source in the mountains.

At first sight, Ueji's gardens look very natural but among the natural rocks, he made very effective use of geometrically shaped stones. However, those designs are not ostentatious at all, they all fade into the garden. In this sense, gardens by Ueji remind me of Japanese kimono designs.

Much more than an artisan, Mr. Ueji was a producer. He had the ability to use the competence of his gardeners to realize the gardens he designed. During his career, he trained numerous gardeners, all of whom have had a great influence on the gardens in Kyoto.

In my family, we've been working on cherry trees for three generations and I planted the big weeping cherry in Maruyama Park."

7 渓谷のはじまりをつげる
3メートルの滝から落ちた疏水の水は
渓流をつくり、船着き場のある
海という池へと流れこむ

The beginning of the stream is a powerful three meter waterfall

さまざまな石の姿は、植治の植治たるところ。素材のおもしろさと自在さを楽しみながら、植治のメッセージを読みとっていただきたい

The essence of Ueji's design: a refined mix of shaped stones and natural rocks

碧雲荘庭園 （野村別邸）

京都市左京区南禅寺下河原町61（非公開）
1917年-28年作庭/20,000m²（約6,000坪）/施主・野村徳七（得庵）

あちこちに佇む
石造物のコレクションは
文化財クラス。
園遊会や茶席の場とも、
能や舞踊の舞台ともなる。
施主の夢を形にした
開放空間に、
植治と息子・白楊の美が
融合する

「碧雲荘」は、大正期の財界の巨頭・野村徳七（得庵）の別荘として1928年に完成している。一応の完成をみるまでに12年を要している。敷地は南禅寺の塔頭跡で、1917年に塚本与三次から購入した。

不動産業の塚本は、京都市の「疏水沿いの地域を含む岡崎と東山一帯の風致保存と宅地化」の方針を受け、別荘地開発と庭付きの高級建売住宅の販売を計画し、土地とともに、水力発電で不要になった疏水沿いの水車の権利、いわゆる水利権をも京都市から買いとっていた。野村は古い建物を修理・改築して翌年に入居し、庭は塚本と連携していた植治に依頼した。

庭は、1917年から1923年までの第一期工事と1928年の第二期工事によって現在の姿になった。第一期工事は長男の白楊が担当。白楊は、東山を借景に舟遊びのできる広大な池と、三つの滝の水を池に導く幅の広い流れをそなえる平安様式の優雅な庭とした。第二期工事は、昭和天皇即位の大礼のさい、碧雲荘が久邇宮邦彦王ご夫妻の宿泊所になるにあたっての改修工事。白楊はすでに死去していて、植治自身が担当した。作庭には、技術とともに人間性と教養がいかに大切かを示した庭でもある。

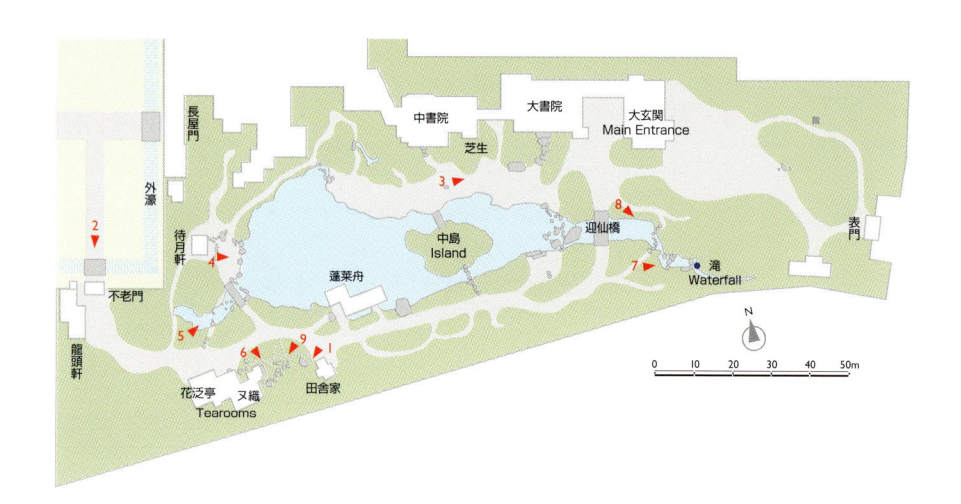

1　得庵のコレクションが景石としてさりげなくおかれている。

The owner NOMURA Tokuan brought ancient engraved rocks into his garden

2　門を抜けて碧雲荘へと誘う橋は、
内と外の世界を遮断するものなのか、
それとも繋ぐものなのか
The bridge that leads into Hekiun-sō garden

Hekiun-sō Garden

Hekiun-sō was the villa of NOMURA Tokushichi II, also known as Tokuan, the founder of the business conglomerate Nomura Zaibatsu.

The garden was created in two phases. Ueji's eldest son, Hakuyō, started to work on it in 1917. Borrowing the Higashiyama hills as background scenery, he created a pond large enough to enjoy boating. The water was drawn from the Lake Biwa Canal. It flows down a three level waterfall at the end of the garden into the pond.

Then in 1928, Hekiun-sō garden was remodeled. At that time, Hakuyō had already died so it was his father, Ueji himself, who was in charge.

In the garden, there are many installations that reflect NOMURA Tokuan's interests including tearooms, a stage for Japanese traditional dance and one for Noh Theater.

6,000坪の敷地の約半分を占める庭には巨大な池があり、舟が浮かぶ。池泉廻遊式の庭を得意とする植治の庭のなかでも、舟が往き来できるのはこの庭くらい。茶人としても知られる得庵らしく、舟上で茶会を開くこともできる。屋内の施設とあわせると茶室だけで7、8軒あり、煎茶席にも使える大きな茶室もそなえている。庭を楽しむ設備も充実していて、珍しいのは大書院を正面にして建てられた能舞台。得庵自身もしばしばここで能を舞った。日本舞踊のための舞台も池に張り出すように設けられていて、先代の井上八千代さんもここで舞った。得庵によって、このように大勢での茶会や園遊会的な食事会、パーティなどに利用できるように工夫された多目的な庭は、古い石造美術や伽藍石などのコレクションを飾る屋外展示場でもある。実業家として成功を収めた得庵の趣味や余技を超えて、日本文化の粋をさまざまなかたちで残し、また再興しようとした得庵の心意気を形にした庭である。

3 住居の前に拡がる芝生。
大きな景石は、腰を下ろすこともできる
A lawn was installed all around the house for garden parties

4 池が山を映し、山もまた庭の一部となる。水鏡が起伏のある遠くを映すことで、透明感のある幽玄さを醸しだしている。池に張り出しているのが踊りの舞台
This lake may be one of the biggest created by Ueji

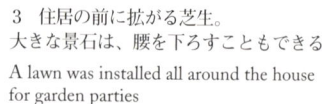

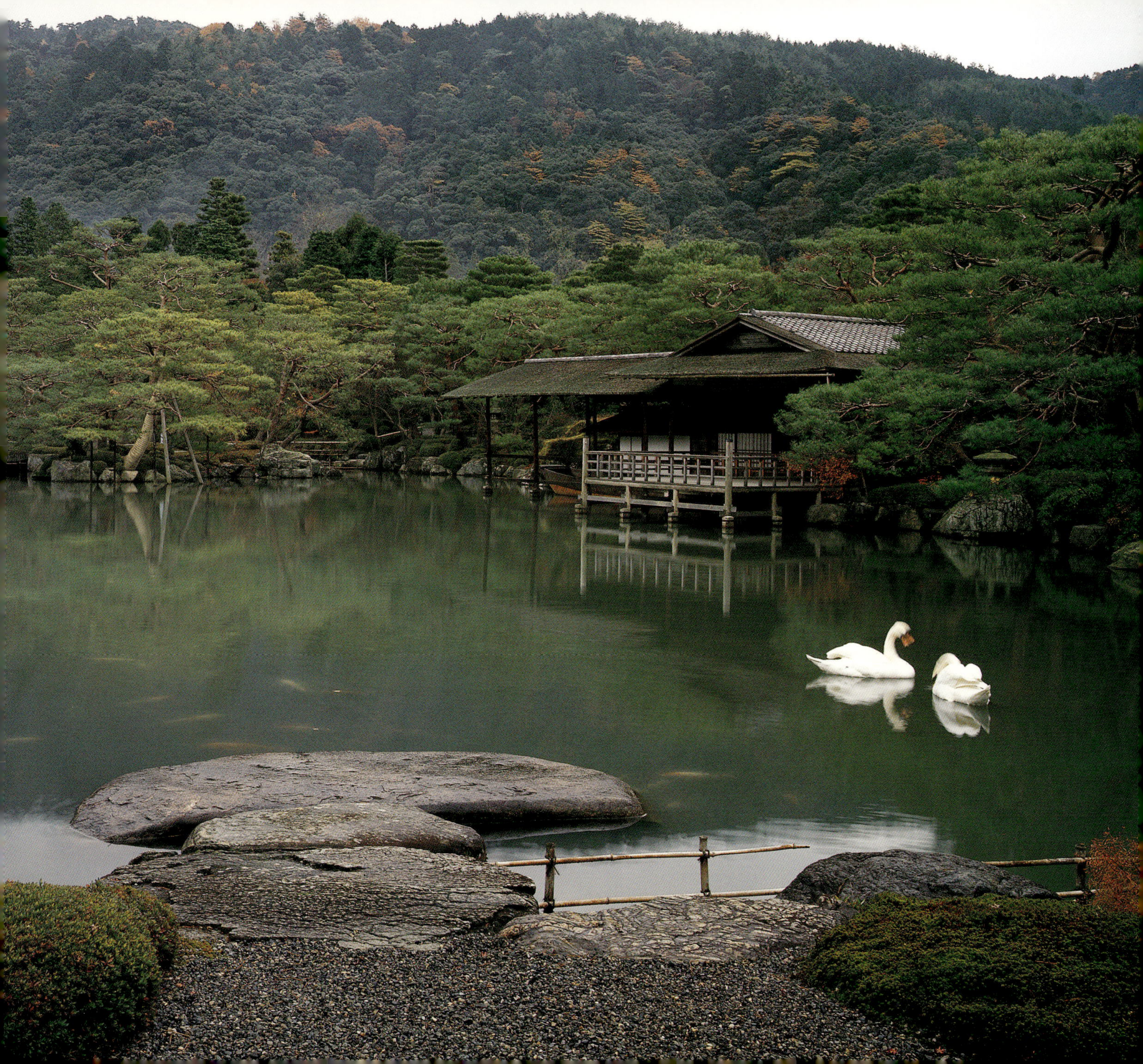

施主・野村徳七（1878-1945）

初代野村徳七の長男として大阪に生まれ、両替商を受け継ぐ。斬新な経営で成功し、やがて野村證券、旧大和銀行など金融と証券を核に野村財閥を形成。1928年には多額納税者として勅選貴族院議員にもなっている。当時は、かつての大名家などが代々の家宝を売りに出した時期。得庵など新興勢力が買い集めた美術品には茶道具もたくさん含まれていた。「茶でもやってみるか」とはじめた茶の湯に、得庵をはじめ多くの財界人がのめり込んだ。当時は「茶の湯もできない人間は、いっぱしの財界人とはいえない」とまで言われた。藪内流の茶の湯を学んだ得庵の約1,500点のコレクションは、隣接する野村美術館が所蔵する。店員に背広を着せ、女子店員を導入するなど西欧化を進める一方で、気息奄々たる日本の伝統芸能を復活させようとしたのが得庵である。

NOMURA Tokushichi II or Tokuan (1875-1945)

Born in Osaka. He inherited an exchange office and created one of the most important business conglomerates in Japan, the Nomura Zaibatsu. He had a great interest in tea ceremony and Noh theater. He was also an avid collector of art and his collection is now on exhibit at the Nomura Art Museum in Kyoto.

◆ In the garden ...
Tani Akira
Curator of the Nomura Art Museum

"The Hekiun-sō villa has two main characteristics. First, it is the largest garden in the Nanzen-ji area. Second, its ownership hasn't changed since it was built.

After the war, the Occupation Army requisitioned a lot of the villas in the vicinity. They painted the wooden walls or even changed the ponds into pools. They made a lot of changes and the villas were damaged. After that, it seems that it was very difficult to return those villas to their former state. I don't know why but Hekiun-sō escaped this requisition. So, the NOMURA family has held Hekiun-sō from generation to generation, and with careful maintenance, the garden has kept its original form.

This is a multipurpose garden, it is filled with many different installations. There are seven or eight tearooms, a Noh theater, and a stage for Japanese traditional dance that extends over the pond. At the time this garden was created, traditional Japanese culture was not higly estimated. I think that within this garden, NOMURA Tokuan tried to create a place to preserve and rebuild Japanese arts and culture. In this way, Hekiun-sō reflects strongly the taste of NOMURA Tokuan. But it can be said that Ueji and his son, Hakuyō, managed to create a garden that surpassed his expectations."

6 庭の一隅におかれている蹲踞には、飛鳥時代の導水設備の一部であったと推定される酒舟石が流用されている。長すぎるために切断した両端は明日香村に残されている

A long hollowed-out stone lead water to the basin

← 5 せせらぎのなかに据えられた流れ蹲踞

The washbasin was placed into the stream creating a refreshing atmosphere

7 秋の色に染まった滝は、植治の世界観・自然観と白楊の洗練された感性の融合のたまもの
The upper part of the three level waterfall covered with maple leaves

8 春の滝。左の秋の滝の写真からは
第一段と第二段が見えるが、
この角度だと三段とも見える。
季節だけでなく眺めるアングルによっても
味わいが違ってくる

The three levels of the waterfall in spring

9 自然石に加工された伽藍石などを混ぜる
植治の得意技。目で楽しませる意匠であると同時に、
足を運ぶ人のリズムをつくる

The rythm of the stepping stones leads the visitors' feet

得庵の夢を庭に開花させた植治

野村美術館学芸部長、茶の湯文化学会会長　谷　晃

碧雲荘の特徴は、南禅寺界隈では最大の庭であること、作庭当初から所有者が変わっていないことです。

戦後、この近辺にあった別荘の多くは進駐軍に接収され、建物にはペンキが塗られ、靴のまま上がれるよう改造され、池はプールになりました。そんな庭や建物を元の姿に戻すのはたいへんです。たまたま接収を免れた碧雲荘は、野村家が代々所有し、10人ほどの庭師が日々手入れすることで作庭当時の姿が保たれています。

この庭ができたころの日本の伝統文化は、元気がありませんでした。古い制度や社会の枠組みは否定され、能や舞、工芸などの伝統もまた価値を失いかけていました。得庵はこの空間にさまざまな日本の文化の粋を集めて保護し、再構築しようと考えたと思われます。この庭はそういう野村得庵の趣味と思想をよく反映しています。

植治と白楊は、得庵が期待した以上にすばらしい庭をつくりあげたのではないでしょうか。

79

高台寺土井庭園（旧十牛庵）

京都市東山区高台寺桝屋町353
1908-1914年作庭/6,600m²（約2,000坪）/施主・清水吉次郎

文化人のサロンとして貴人、文人、画家たちを
迎える大阪商人の別荘「十牛庵」。
その十牛庵を任されたのが数寄屋の上坂と植治。
水と石の魔術師・植治は、水がなければどうするか

清水吉次郎
SHIMIZU Kichijirō

近代京都の別荘建築に大きな足跡を残した「十牛庵」は、明治後期から昭和初期にかけて活躍した大阪の実業家、清水吉次郎の別荘として普請された。清水家は大阪で代々「油屋」を名乗った両替商。その六代目の吉次郎は、商才発揮というより先代の蓄えで人生を楽しんだ人。

植治とは因縁めいた関わりを示す。清水が京都で最初に手に入れたのは、のちに植治が作庭することになる對龍山荘の土地、次いで山縣有朋も所有したかつての角倉了以の邸宅。1906年にこれを売却した清水は、東山山裾のこの地を入手する。大きな住宅と茶亭の工事を請け負ったのは当時、数寄屋の名工とうたわれた上坂浅次郎。

明治の終わりころの十牛庵は、文化人のサロン。歌人の池辺義象や画家の浅井忠、津田青楓らが集まって光琳会をもよおすなど、一時代を画した。清水以後、所有者は転々とし、1953年に料亭として開業。この間、建物にも庭にも手が加えられた。

Kōdaiji-Doi Garden

Kōdaiji-Doi was the former residence of a businessman from Osaka, SHIMIZU Kichijirō. At the time, it was called Jyūgyū-an. The SHIMIZU family owned an exchange house in Osaka and had a great fortune. Thanks to his family fortune Kichijirō could enjoy life in Kyoto and created many villas where he held literary salons. Jyūgyū-an was one of those villas. He bought this site on the slope of the Higashiyama hills in 1906 and asked Ueji to create the garden. In 1953 it became a Japanese-style restaurant and changed its name to Kōdaiji-Doi.

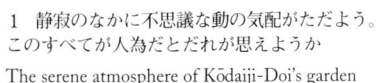

1　静寂のなかに不思議な動の気配がただよう。このすべてが人為だとだれが思えようか
The serene atmosphere of Kōdaiji-Doi's garden

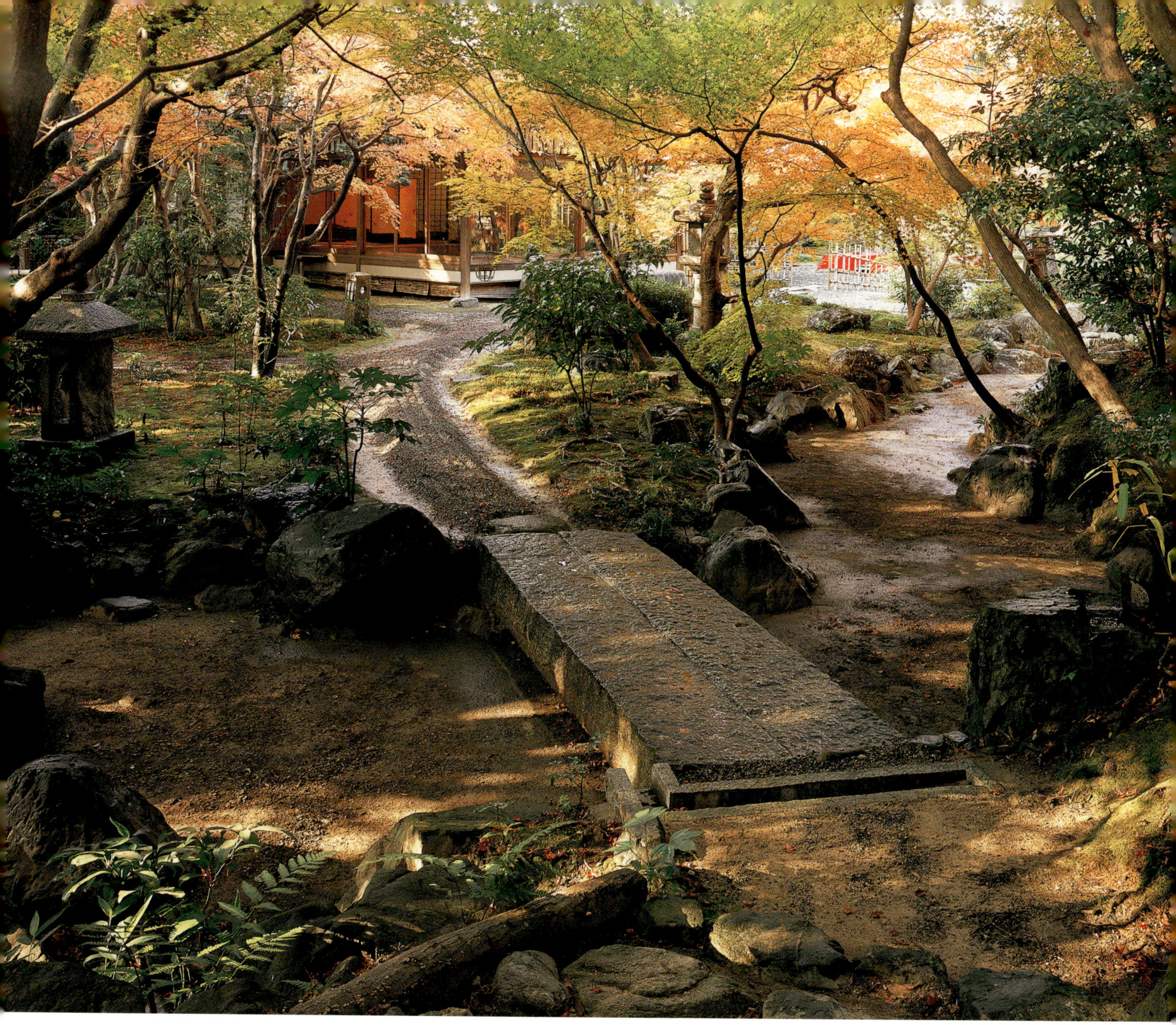

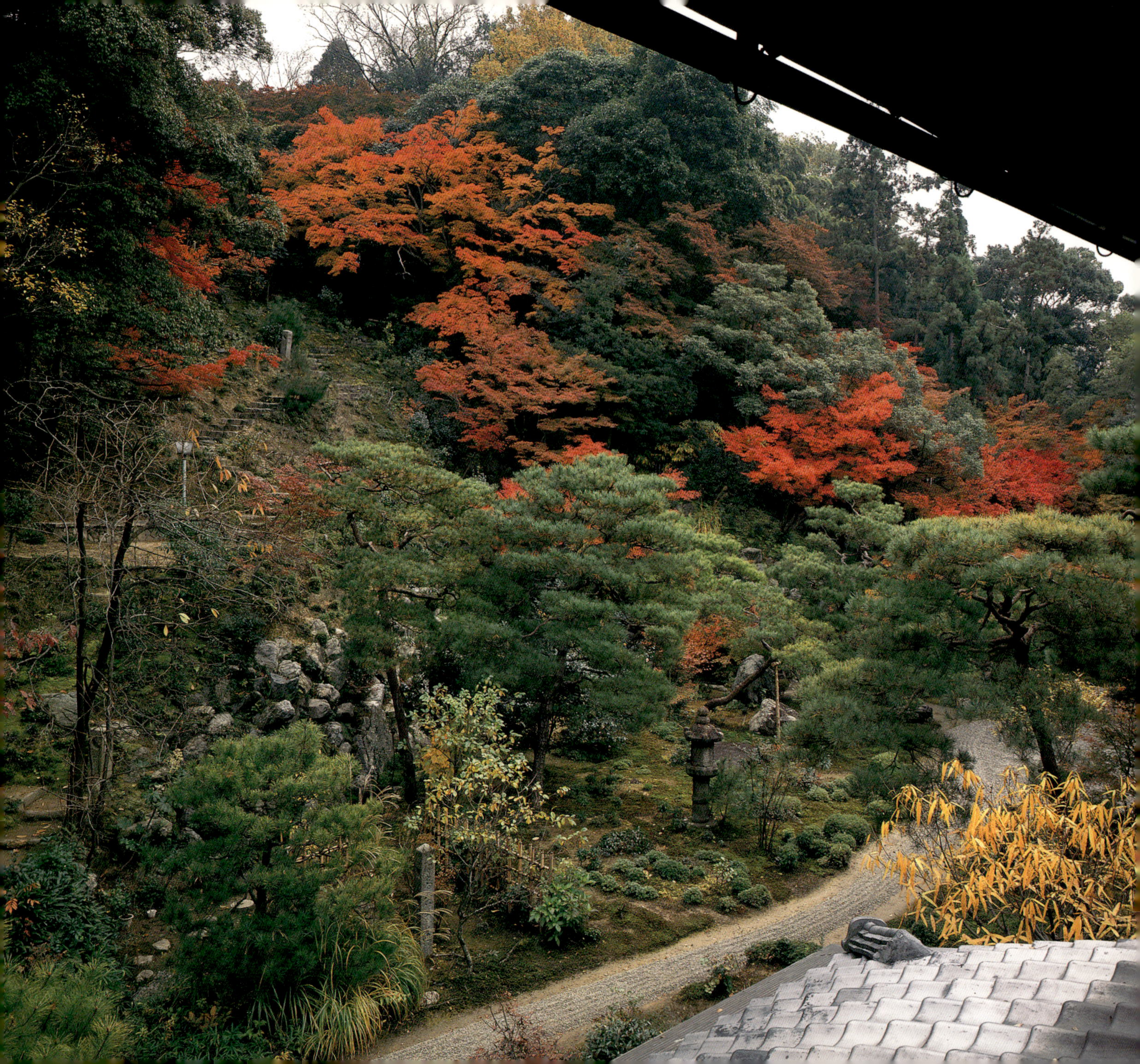

2 二階から山裾の緑を望む。100年前の植治の作意を理解しつつ、成長する樹木にどう手を入れるかは現代の庭師の感性に任される

Kōdaiji-Doi garden was created on a steep slope

3 座敷から前庭を眺める。いまは黒い砂利を敷いた枯山水調だが、植治は芝生の空間にしていたという

Originally, it was not gravel but a lawn that was laid out in front of the reception room

八坂神社と清水寺のあいだの東山を少し登った山裾に位置する高台寺土井。庭は、西向きの斜面を利用して三段で構成。最上段からは京都のまちが眺望できる。眼前には八坂の塔がそびえる。

植治は中段から下段にかけて渓流を表現しているが、さすがに疏水の水は引けず、枯滝から枯池へとつなぐ枯山水とした。

大正天皇即位の大礼の前年の1914年にも、上坂と植治の手で大規模に改造された。十牛庵が貴族院議員の宿泊所に選定されたことが理由だが、清水は納得のゆくまで自らの美意識を庭に映し込みたかったようだ。石を動かし、樹木を植えかえる日々を楽しんだ。

Kōdaiji-Doi is located between the famous Kiyomizu-dera temple and Yasaka-jinja shrine, at the foot of the Higashiyama hills. The garden was created on three levels on a steep slope. It was impossible to draw water up so high so, uniquely for him, Ueji designed a dry stream and waterfall. Today water flows through Ueji's design but there was no need to change his perfectly constructed stone setting.

4　自然石と加工石とを調和させる
　　植治得意の蹲踞。
　　石燈籠を少し離しておくことで
　　奥行きの深さ、遠近感を強調する
A crouching basin arrangement at the entrance of the reception room

5　四阿は茶室としても使われる
A peculiar lantern without pillar

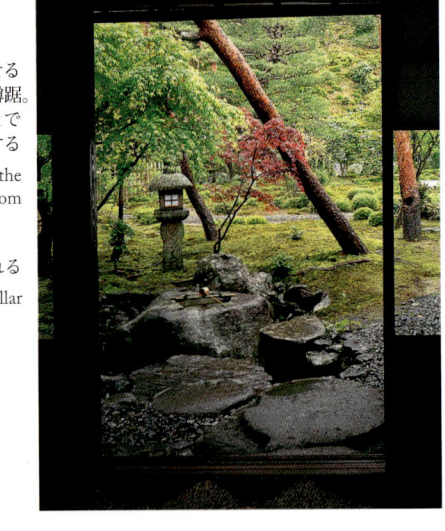

6　3本の円柱石に波打つ枝の紅葉を組みあわせた
　　縁先手水鉢。石燈籠の位置がその役割と効果を
　　意識させる
A washbasin composition of three pillars close to the veranda

「用」を備えた枯流れは、植治の真骨頂でしょう

矢ヶ崎善太郎
京都工芸繊維大学大学院准教授

初めて訪れてまず驚いたのは、「水がない」こと。植治の庭にはかならず滝や池、流れがあって水は欠かせないものとばかり思っていました。建物はわずかな平坦部に建ち、庭は急な斜面地にあります。植治はここに枯滝と枯流れをつくっていますが、まったく水が流れないということでもないんですよ。雨水の排水路としての機能があるんです。無鄰菴の防火用水や並河靖之七宝記念館の研磨用水のように、必要があって取り込んだ水を庭に利用するという植治の合理性にもとづいているんですね。急斜面に建てた建物や庭の構造上、雨水をいちはやく排出する必要があったわけで、「用」に応じた石組みとしながら、渓流の自然な風景をつくりだす。いかにも植治らしいですね。

庭の最上段からは、八坂の塔越しに京都盆地を一望するダイナミックな眺めが楽しめます。岡崎一帯に多くある植治の庭は東山を見上げるのが共通する構図ですが、この庭は東山から京都盆地を望むことができるのが特徴です。清水吉次郎の養女の久さんにお会いしたときに聞いたのですが、「こうするとミミズがあがってこないんだ」といって、吉次郎さんはムクロジの実の煮汁を松の根の周りに撒いておられたそうです。植治さんから教わったのでしょう。

枯滝と枯流れは、お客さまの要望で、いまは時間を決めて水を流されるそうです。

7　数寄屋造りの繊細で瀟洒な屋根が豊かな緑に埋もれる。視線を上げると八坂の塔越しに京都盆地が一望できる
Panoramic view of Kyoto city from the highest level of the garden

9　枯滝といえども雨の日には雨水が
流れるように構成されている

Even though it is a dry landscape, Ueji's
design is not abstract but remains
always natural

8・10　枯滝の石組みの春と秋。
植治の植栽がつくる季節感は、
水がなくても表情豊か

The dry waterfall was designed to
channel rain water down the slope

◆ **In the garden ...**
YAGASAKI Zentarō
Professor at Kyoto Institute of Technology

"The first thing that caught my eye when I saw the Kōdaiji-Doi garden was that there was no water. All Ueji's gardens I had seen up to that point invariably had a waterfall, a stream and a pond. I thought that "water" was the keyword for Ueji's gardens.

This garden was created on a very steep slope. Ueji created a dry stream and a dry waterfall, but it doesn't mean that there is no water at all. Actually, this stone arrangement functions to channel the rainwater down the slope. In Kōdaiji-Doi, Ueji couldn't draw water but still, his garden design answered a special need. Ueji's gardens are not abstract, they are always very functional, and even though they are functional, they always look very natural; maybe this is the fundamental characteristic of Ueji's gardens.

From the upper level of the garden, you have the Tower of Yasaka in the foreground and behind it the whole Kyoto basin. It's a very impressive panorama. It's interesting to note that all the other gardens by Ueji in the Okazaki and Nanzen-ji area borrow the Higashiyama hills as background scenery but in Kōdaiji-Doi it's the opposite, you can stare at Kyoto city from the Higashiyama hills."

「葵殿庭園」と「佳水園庭園」（ウェスティン都ホテル京都）

京都市東山区粟田口華頂町1
作庭・1925年（白楊）、1933年（植治）／施主・都ホテル、清浦奎吾

**植治の技法、信念を
もっともよく理解したのが
息子・白楊。そして、
若くしてその遺作となった
のが「佳水園庭園」。
植治にとっても、
同じホテルの庭が
最後の仕事となった**

華頂山の斜面に沿って階段状に延びるウェスティン都ホテル京都。蹴上浄水場に隣接し、北向きの部屋からは、右手にインクラインと琵琶湖疏水を挟んで南禅寺を眺望し、無鄰庵と琵琶湖疏水記念館を正面の眼下におく。前身の「吉水苑」は、京都の近代化の震源となったこの地に、第一期疏水工事が竣工した年に開業。その10年後の1900年には、「都ホテル」に改名している。植治による「葵殿庭園」と、植治の長男の白楊による「佳水園庭園」がある。

葵殿庭園は、大正天皇即位の御大典が京都であった1915年に建てられた宴会場「葵殿」に、植治が1933年に疏水の水をもちいて、流れ、滝、池で構成した庭。植治の遺作。

佳水園庭園は、元は内閣総理大臣も務めた清浦奎吾伯爵のかつての別荘「喜寿庵」の庭で、当時の都ホテルに隣接していた。白楊が1925年に作庭したものの、白楊はその翌年に43歳で病没。

植治、白楊の最後の仕事になった因縁の二つの庭は、やがて敷地を拡張したホテルの所有となった。白楊の喜寿庵には和風の別館が建てられて「佳水園」と改名。白砂と芝生で瓢箪をデザインした現在の中庭は、白楊ではなく建築家の村野藤吾の仕事で、1990年から3年をかけて尼﨑博正氏が修理した。

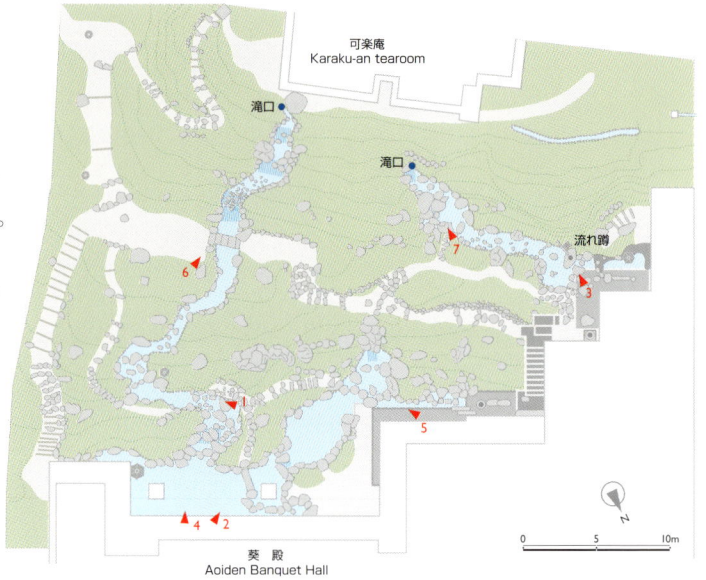

佳水園の滝（葵殿から遠く離れているため、図は省略）
Detail of the Kasuien waterfall designed by Ueji's eldest son, Hakuyō

Westin Miyako Kyoto Gardens

The Westin Miyako Kyoto is an hotel located next to the Lake Biwa Canal and Nanzen-ji temple. It opened its doors in 1900. In the hotel, there are two gardens, the Aoiden Garden created by Ueji and the Kasuien Garden created by Ueji's eldest son, Hakuyō.

The Kasuien Garden was formerly a part of the villa of Count KIYOURA Keigo. Hakuyō created it in 1925 and it later became a part of the hotel. Hakuyō died suddenly one year after the completion of this garden.

The Aoiden banquet hall was built in 1915. Originally, there was no garden but in 1933, drawing water from the Lake Biwa Canal, Ueji created a stream and a waterfall in front of the banquet hall. For Ueji too, Aoiden Garden was a posthumously completed work.

1　山に分け入るさまを再現した渓流にある沢飛石は、無骨な自然のようでいて、人の歩みをやさしく計算している〈葵殿〉

Stepping stones crossing the stream in the Aoiden Garden

植治は1904年にホテル入り口に滝を設けたものの、その後の依頼は途絶えていたようだ。しかし、山裾の斜面に建つホテルの上層部に茶室「可楽庵」が1933年に設けられたことをきっかけに、植治は「可楽庵露地」と「葵殿庭園」を作庭する。露地は樹木に囲まれ、そこを水が軽快に流れる。茶室にふさわしく山居の雰囲気がただよう。「葵殿庭園」の中心は高低差15メートルほどもある雄大な3段の滝で、「雲井の滝」は清浦伯爵の命名。清浦伯爵もまた、山縣有朋に近い政治家であった。

葵殿の南側と北側には大きなガラス窓がたてられ、その向こうに庭が透ける。欄間には京都の三大祭り、葵祭・祇園祭・時代祭を題材にするステンドグラスがはまる。

工事は、植治が死去した翌年に終わった。ホテルの入り口近くにあった植治の滝は、1985年に撤去された。

2 加工石と自然石とが共存する沢飛石〈葵殿〉
Ueji liked to mix shaped rocks with stepping stones

3 水の流れに溶けこむ蹲踞〈葵殿〉
This washbasin extends into the stream

4 「葵殿庭園」、雲井の滝の下段。琵琶湖西岸で産出される守山石が多量に使用されている。刈り込まれて散在するサツキと美しい調和をつくる
Overview of the Aoiden Garden from the banquet hall

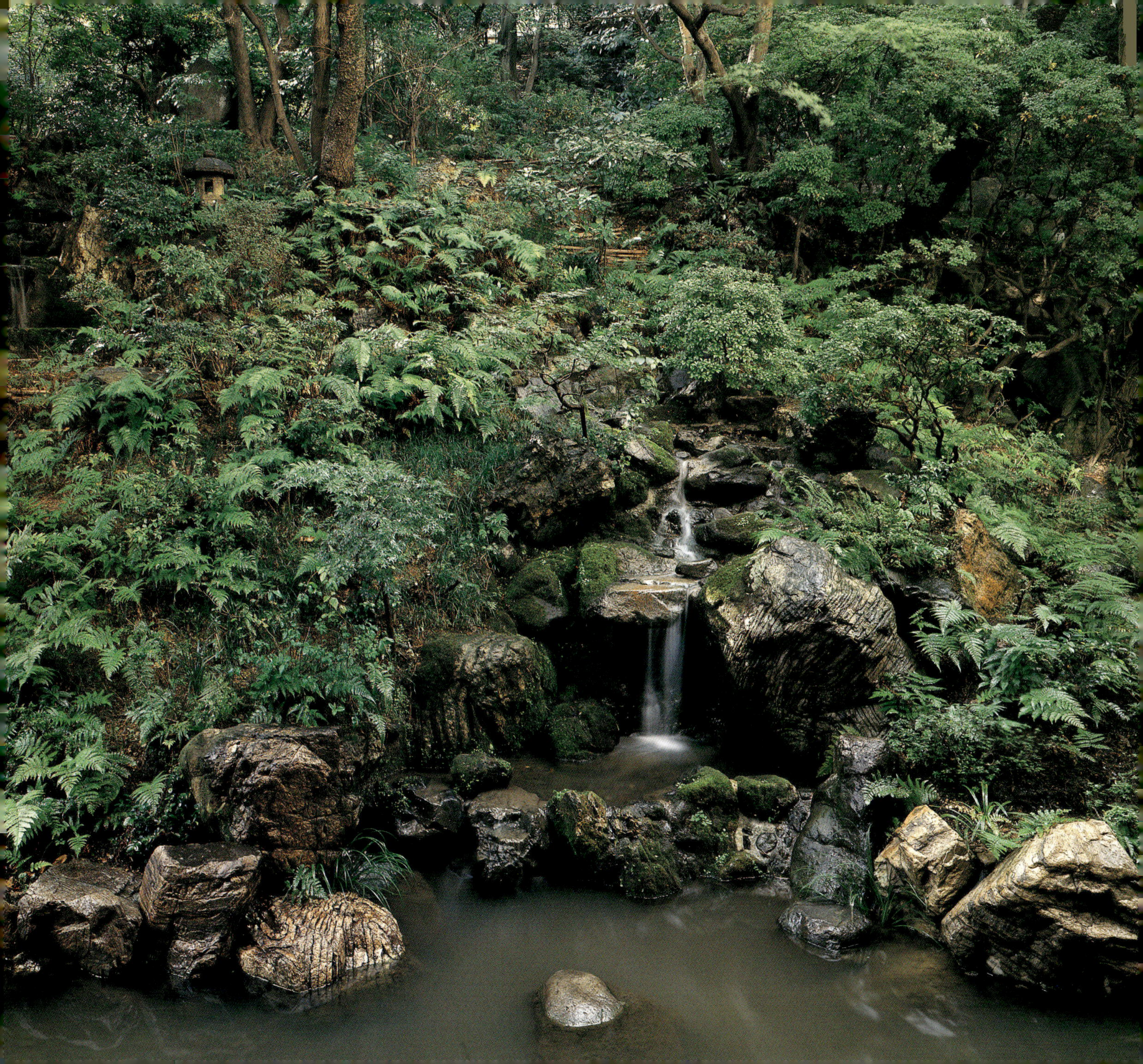

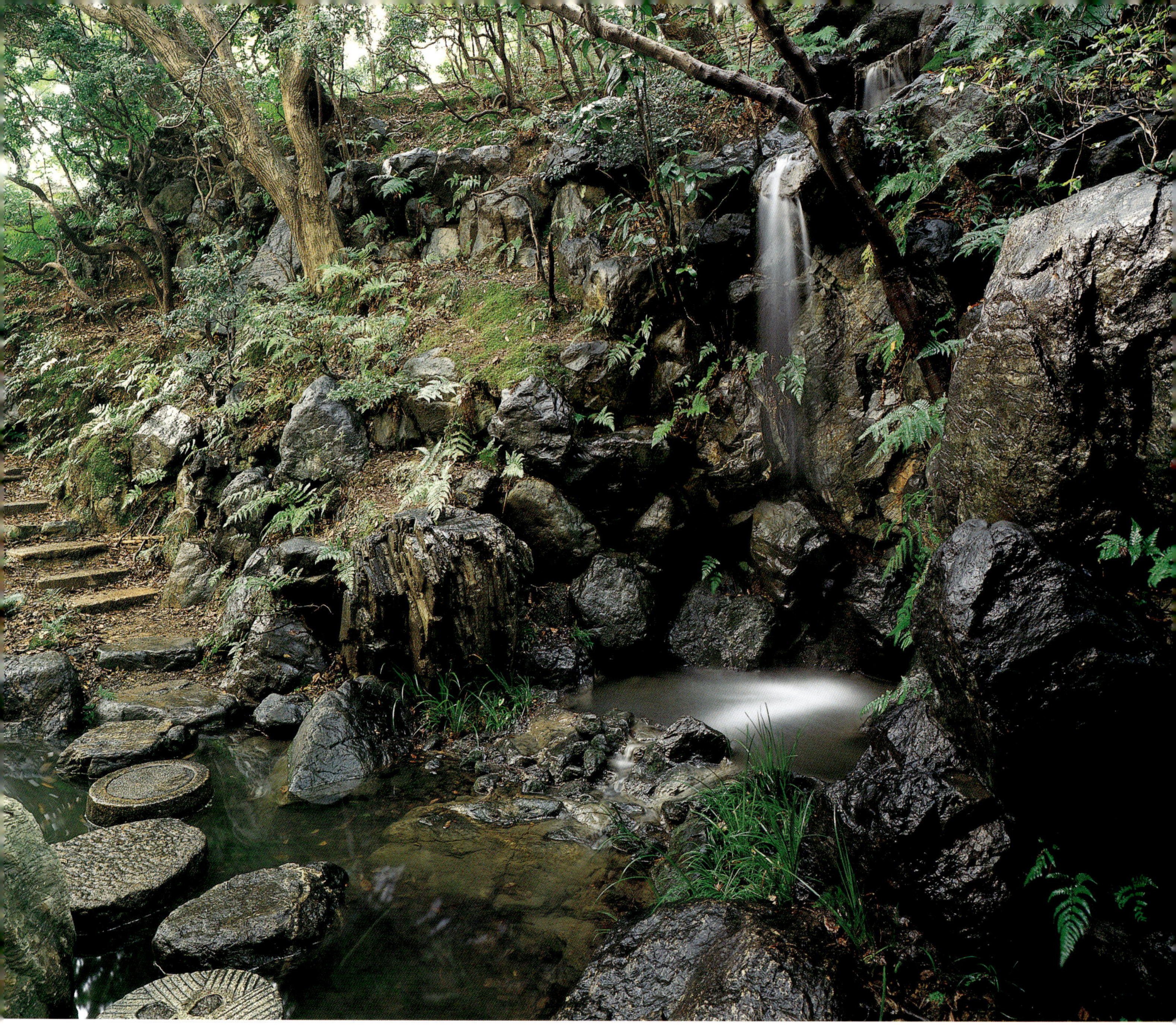

6 突如として現れる加工石の石橋は、違和感ではなく安堵感を与える。
山裾の滝は、雲井の滝の上段にあたり、中段の滝をへて
91ページの下段の滝へとつながる

This man-made bridge contrasts with the natural waterfall

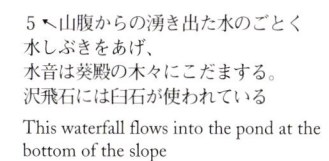

7 葵殿の滝岩組。人はなにに自然を感じるのか

The huge yellow stone that supports the waterfall is called a "mirror stone"

5 山腹からの湧き出た水のごとく
水しぶきをあげ、
水音は葵殿の木々にこだまする。
沢飛石には臼石が使われている

This waterfall flows into the pond at the bottom of the slope

The Aoiden Garden is a long waterfall flowing down a 15 meter slope. It starts at the bottom of the Karaku-an tearoom and goes down in three levels to the pond, in front of the Aoiden banquet hall. This is Ueji's last creation. He created many waterfalls, each of them very different but always very natural, surrounded by a lot of greenery.

It's possible to enjoy this garden by walking along its winding path or through the large windows while sitting in the Aoiden banquet hall.

♦ In the garden ...
Sasaoka Ryūho
Master of ikebana, Japanese flower arrangement

"The present Kasuien garden is composed of two creations: the stream flowing down a natural rock was created by the son of Ueji, Hakuyō, and the gourd-shape design with white gravel and lawn was created by MURANO Tōgo afterwards. To get to the Kasuien garden, you take the elevator up to the seventh floor, go through a corridor and then exit the building. My first impression was, "power." I was overwhelmed by the strong presence of the rugged rock. But when I got to the end of the garden, I discovered this very sweet gourd-shaped design. Those two creations form a very good contrast and give this garden an interesting dynamic.

This garden is a very good stimulus for creativity and it makes me think about my art. Here, Hakuyō combined the roughness of natural stone with the refined lines of the water drawn from the Lake Biwa Canal. The garden creations by Ueji, who made good use of all the natural elements of the surroundings: water, plants, rocks, etc; have something in common with the spirit of ikebana. The art of ikebana consists of finding the best way to present flowers that were cut in nature. As we feel nostalgic in front of a village in the mountains, I think the charm of this garden is that it has both natural beauty and human warmth."

佳水園庭園の岩肌をくねくねと
這うように流れ落ちる水も疏水の水
The water flows very gently over this impressive rock

白楊遺作の佳水園庭園には
植治のなかに
白楊がいるようであり、
白楊のなかに
植治がいるようでもある

Kasuien garden was the last creation of the brilliant but too short career of Ueji's eldest son, Hakuyō

いけばなに通じる植治と白楊の自然観

笹岡隆甫
華道「未生流笹岡」次期家元

現在の佳水園庭園には、植治の長男の白楊が手がけた庭と、建築家の村野藤吾が白砂と芝生で構成した瓢箪の庭の二つがあります。ホテル内のエレベーターで7階まで上がり、廊下を進むとそこに自然の山肌を利用した庭が現れます。傾斜地に建つこのホテルならではの仕掛けがおもしろい。佳水園と出会った第一印象は、「力強さ」。斜面の山肌に露出する岩の迫力に圧倒されます。ゴツゴツした無骨な岩肌に愛らしい瓢箪。この好対照が不思議な魅力をかもし出しています。

ところが、さらに進むと、瓢箪と杯をモチーフにした愛らしい庭が現れます。この庭は、私に花を生ける心構えを思い出させてくれます。白楊は佳水園で、自然の岩場と疏水の水をみごとに取り込んでいます。水や植物、石など、「そこにある自然をどのように生かすか」を問いかける植治の庭づくりは、野山に咲く花を切り取って身近な場所で楽しむ「いけばなの精神」にも通じるんですね。

華道家も、どうすれば花のよさが引き立つかと苦心し、技巧を凝らします。私たちは野性の自然ではなく、手入れされた田んぼや里山に郷愁を覚える。人がつくりこんだものにこそ味わいがある。私たちはこの庭に、人の手の温もりを発見するからこそ、自然なやすらぎを感じるのです。

94

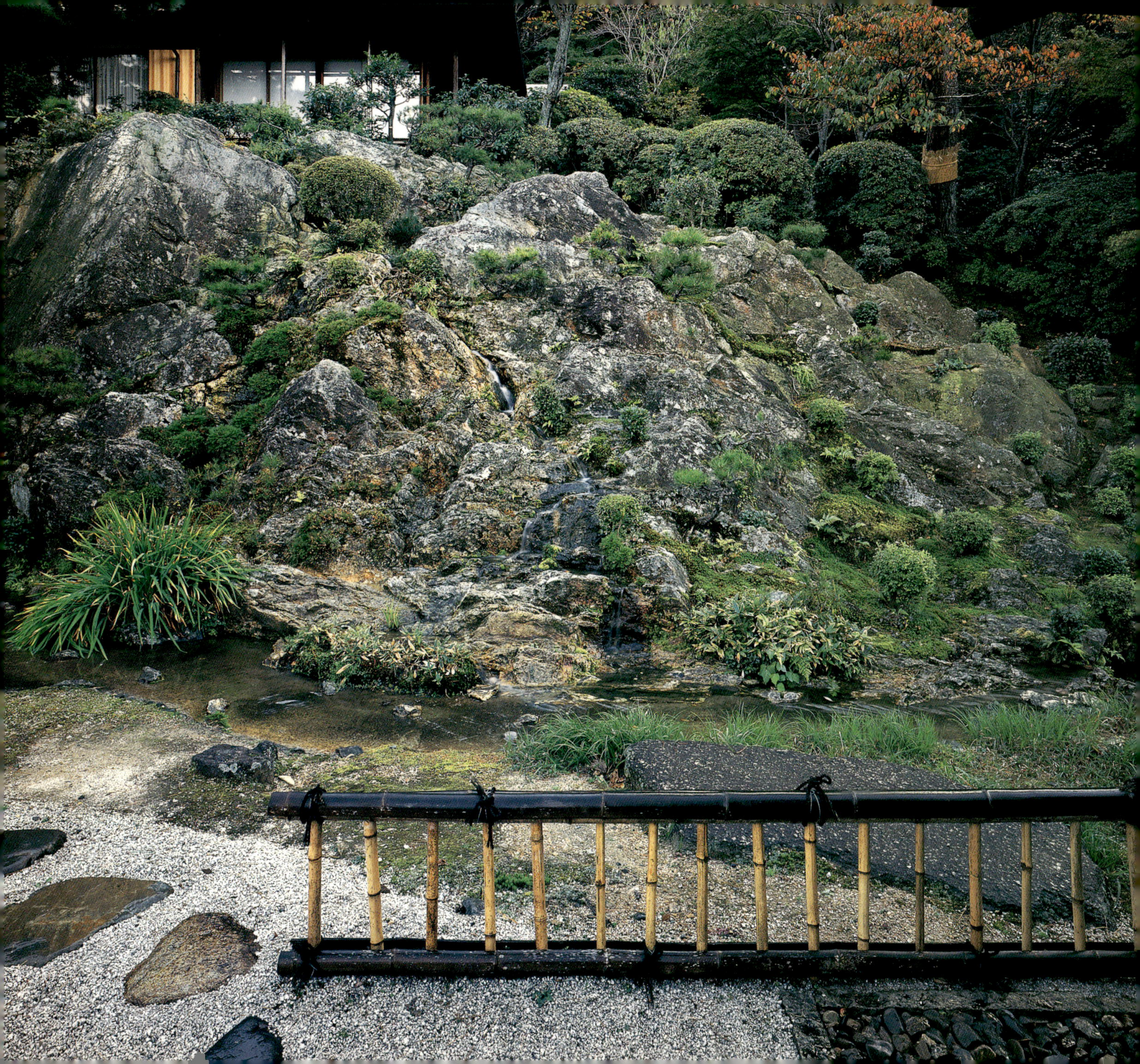

文化的景観としての植治の「自然」
Creating Nature: Ueji and Kyoto Culture

「水と石の魔術師」と評される卓抜した表現力と革新性をそなえた植治。維新という革命をへた植治の時代は、新しいものを受け入れることに躊躇しない変革の時代。欧米の事情を視野に入れつつ行動する山縣有朋ら政財界人と出会った植治は、異文化を知ることで逆に、日本の伝統文化と美意識にアイデンティティを求めた。そのうえで、公共空間の日本庭園化など、新しい京都庭園の枠組みをあみだした植治の庭とはなんであったのか、その美意識を支えた思想とは。植治の活躍の足跡をたどるとともに、今日的意義を検証する

出席
白幡洋三郎　国際日本文化研究センター教授
笹岡隆甫　未生流笹岡家元嗣
谷　晃　野村美術館学芸部長、茶の湯文化学会会長
永田　萠　イラストレーター、絵本作家

Present:
SHIRAHATA Yōzaburō (Professor, International Center for Japanese Researches)
TANI Akira (Curator, Nomura Art Museum)
NAGATA Moe (Illustrator)
SASAOKA Ryūho (Master of ikebana, Japanese flower arrangement)

2007年10月15日、無鄰庵の階上にて
This discussion was held on the 15th October 2007, in Murin-an

白幡●無鄰庵の二階からだと借景の東山が大きく見えますね。植治は庭木として当時珍しかったモミの木をこの庭に30本ほど植えたと言います。垂直の線が強調されるモミの木はこの庭園にどのような印象を与えていたのでしょうか。東山を尊重することがこの庭の造園の要諦だとしたら、モミもきっとその借景効果に貢献したはずです。植治が100年先のいまの姿をどう考えていたか知りませんが、木もずいぶん大きくなっている。

谷●樹木が成長することは、あるていど計算しているんでしょうけれどね。

白幡●40年ぐらい先までは考えると思うが、100年先までは考えにくい。モミの木も枯れて、いまはありません。しかし施主の山縣有朋は「この庭園の主山は東山だ」と言っていますから、植治はその考えにあわせて樹木を選んだはずです。

谷●最近はマツクイムシで松が枯れることが多いのですが、枯れ木を切り倒すと眺めが一変することがありますね。

永田●でも、この庭は天然の自然に少し手を加えたというレベルではありませんよね。画家が白いキャンバスに向かうように、植治の自然観を元にデッサンされたのだと思います。そういう全体をつかまえる画家と同じ眼差しをこの庭から感じます。木が伸びたり枯れたりすると構図までが狂ってしまうようなお庭ではなく、人を包み込み、時代の変化を受け止める、そういう大きな輪郭を感じます。

笹岡●私は、この無鄰庵で花を生けたことがあります。無鄰庵には遠景があって、その手前に水の流れがあります。そこで、さらにその手前に水を張ってカキツバタを生け、近景を演出しました。繊細でやさしいこの庭に、いけばなはよく似あうんです。石組みよりも植栽が中心で、水がたおやかに流れる、ほんとうに落ち着く空間。借景の手法を取り入れながら遠近感を強く押し出して、まさに京都らしい庭園と言えますね。

明治・大正期の最高の庭師

白幡●近代日本の黎明期の明治という時代に生きて、西洋の文化・文明と接触しつつ日本の庭のあり方を考えたのが植治です。きょうは茶、花、絵の専門家にお集まりいただきましたが、そういう植治はどのように捉えられるのか、それぞれの分野からご意見をうかがうことで、植治の庭に新たな接近ができるのではないかと期待しています。

ただし、植治がどういう仕事をしたのか、その事績の全体はよくわかっていません。どの庭に植治が関係したかぐらいはわかっても、細部はわかっていない。それでもやはり、植治は明治・大正期にもっとも活躍した庭師です。その植治の考え方・美学は、近代の日本庭園の重要な構成要素となっていると思います。

谷●私がいる野村美術館の隣に、野村證券などの金融グループを築いた野村徳七の別荘「碧雲荘」があって、庭園は通常「植治の庭」と言われます。6,000坪ありますが、現在の小川家の当主、十一代目植治の話を聞くと、植治よりも息子の白楊が関与した度合いが高いのではないかと。そうはいっても、植治の特徴が随所に見られる庭ですが。

しかし、茶の湯の世界だと、たとえば

●*SHIRAHATA*: From the second floor of Murin-an villa (see p. 30-41), the background scenery, the Higashiyama hills, look much bigger than from the ground floor! The trees have grown a great deal. I wonder what Ueji thought about the evolution of this garden when he created it, one hundred years ago.

●*TANI*: I guess that, in some measure, the growth of the trees was taken into account.

●*SHIRAHATA*: It is possible to imagine the growth of trees over a span of 40 years but I think it's more difficult over a span of 100 years.

●*TANI*: Recently, pine trees throughout Japan are being attacked by worms and they die easily. When you cut the pine trees down in a garden, the view changes radically.

●*NAGATA*: I don't think this garden was created by just rearranging a corner of Nature. As a painter expresses himself on a white canvas, this garden is the result of Ueji's artistic sense. Like a painter thinking of the whole surface of his canvas, this garden was created with a holistic vision of the individual elements. I can sense a form of framing here. The structure of this garden won't change because the trees grow or die.

●*SASAOKA*: I've already arranged flowers in Murin-an. In this garden, there is already a background with the water flowing nearby. What I did was to create a foreground with irises. This refined and friendly garden is perfect for ikebana. The vivid green of the plants, the murmuring of the stream; Murin-an is a place where you can relax.

Ueji, The Finest Landscape Designer of the Meiji Era (1868-1912)

●*SHIRAHATA*: Ueji was active during the Meiji era, the dawn of modernization. Japan opened its frontiers and had to integrate the culture and the new techniques of the Occident. In this context, Ueji had to think about what the modern Japanese garden should be.

Today, sitting around this table, there is one specialist in tea ceremony, one in ikebana and one in painting. By studying Ueji's gardens from those different points of view, I hope we will discover a new approach to understanding his creations. Actually, there is not much information left about Ueji and his works. Even if we know about some of the gardens he was involved in, we know very little about his work in detail. Still, Ueji is the most famous landscape gardener of the Meiji era.

茶室を建てる場合、大工の棟梁が「こうしましょう」と決めるのではなく、施主の意見を充分に聞いたうえで施主の考えを実現させるのが一般的です。庭園をつくるにあたっても、野村徳七はそういう指導をしたのではないでしょうか。
笹岡●すると、碧雲荘は植治よりも白楊あるいは施主の徳七さんの想いのほうが強く出ているのですか。
谷●そうだと思います。しかし、施主の意向をいくら汲んでも、職人さんにはそれぞれ自己主張がありますからね。

施主の想いをつむぎ、形にする

谷●徳七は「得庵」という号をもっていて、趣味の世界では得庵。得庵はたいへんな多趣味で、なかでも茶の湯と能にのめり込みます。したがって当初は、この二つを柱に碧雲荘を構想したのではないかと考えていたわけです。事実、茶室として使える建物あるいは部屋が七つ八つあって、能舞台もあります。得庵自身も、そこで茶の湯をやったり能を演じたりして

白幡洋三郎 しらはた・ようざぶろう
1949年、大阪府に生まれる。京都大学大学院博士課程単位取得退学、農学博士。造園学・産業技術史専攻。主な著書に、『プラントハンター――ヨーロッパの植物熱と日本』、『近代都市公園史の研究――欧化の系譜』、『大名庭園――江戸の饗宴』、『庭園の美・造園の心――ヨーロッパと日本』、『造園を読む――ランドスケープの四季』(共著)、『都林泉名勝図会――京都の名所名園案内』などがある。

SHIRAHATA Yōzaburō
Born in 1948, in Osaka. Graduated from Kyoto University, Doctor of Agriculture. His major was the history of landscape gardening and industrial techniques. He is now a professor at the International Research Center for Japanese Studies.

楽しんでいたようです。
けれども、最近になって、かならずしも茶の湯と能のための庭園だったのではなくて、茶の湯を柱に、当時は息もたえだえだった日本文化を再構築しようという意図があったのではないかと考えるようになりました。その夢をかなえるには庭をどうすべきかという意向が働き、その結果がこの庭園ではないかと。ですから、この庭園は野村得庵個人の好みがかなり反映されています。
白幡●碧雲荘には大きな池があって、池に浮かぶ舟もまた茶室になっていますね。
谷●ええ、基本的には池泉廻遊式*の庭園で、池を穿って舟を浮かべています。得庵の頭の中には平安時代の宮廷の竜頭鷁首(りょうとうげき)の船、船遊びのイメージがあったんでしょうけれども、得庵は竜頭鷁首にせず、屋形船の上に茶室を載せた。藪内の家元にある茶室をそのまま写して載せて、舟を動かしながら茶の湯を楽しむ趣向です。これは得庵の発想だろうと思いますね。
白幡●植治も茶の湯を……。
谷●もちろん嗜んでいたと思います。だからこそ、得庵の意向を汲むことができる。茶の湯をまったく知らなければ、あるいは能を知らなければ、そういった意向は実現できないわけですからね。
白幡●しかし、船を浮かべてという発想は、やっぱり得庵のアイデア。それを実現するにはどうすればよいかを二人で考えたということですね。
谷●もう一つの特徴は、池にせり出した舞台があること。先代の井上八千代さんもしばしばここで舞を披露されました。
白幡●池に舟を浮かべての茶というのは、

Obviously, Ueji's aesthetic sense had a strong influence on the development of the modern Japanese garden.
●*TANI*: Next to the Nomura Art Museum, where I work, is the Hekiun-sō villa, owned by the Nomura Group Companies. It is generally said that the Hekiun-sō garden (see p. 72-79) is Ueji's creation, but his successor, OGAWA Jihei XI, said that it is much more the work of his son, Hakuyō. However, the characteristics of Ueji's gardens are present.

In the world of tea ceremony, for example, when you build a tearoom, it is not the carpenter who decides; first he listens to the owner's idea and then he uses his skill to realize it. I think it's the same when you create a garden. I think that the owner NOMURA Tokuan gave the instructions for the construction of the Hekiun-sō garden.
●*SASAOKA*: So, could it be said that the Hekiun-sō garden is a creation of Tokuan?
●*TANI*: In a sense, yes. But even if they have to take into account the intentions of the owner, craftsmen can still assert themselves within those constraints.

The Owner's Intent
●*TANI*: NOMURA Tokuan, the owner of Hekiun-sō was a person with a wide range of interests. He was particularly absorbed in tea ceremony and Noh Theater, which are well represented in the Hekiun-sō garden. There are seven or eight tearooms and a stage for Noh Theater. Tokuan himself enjoyed performing tea ceremony and Noh there.

However, I recently started to believe that this garden was not only for tea ceremony and Noh Theater. At the time it was created, Japanese culture was stagnating and I think that Tokuan's intention was to give a new lift to traditional Japanese arts. This is why this garden reflects much of the taste of the owner Tokuan.
●*SHIRAHATA*: In the garden, there is a large pond with a boat made to look like a tearoom, isn't there?
●*TANI*: Yes, Hekiun-sō garden has a pond deep enough for a boat. I think that Tokuan had an image of the gardens of the aristocrats in ancient times, but he did not create a simple copy of those ancient gardens. On the boat, he created a tearoom for the enjoyment of tea ceremony while floating. This is one of Tokuan's ideas.
●*SHIRAHATA*: Do you think Ueji also knew about tea ceremony?

ほかにないんじゃないかな。こんなスケールの植治の庭は碧雲荘だけでしょう。
谷●たぶんあの庭だけだと思いますね。

創造性は、なにによって生まれるのか

笹岡●植治と重森三玲とでは時代はずいぶん違いますが、よく比較されますね。三玲の大胆さにたいして、植治は繊細。石組みと植栽との違いでしょうか。

永田●私は三玲の庭も大好きです。まさにデザインの極致で、人の存在なんか無用だと思わせる。観客が庭に加わることは拒否、拒絶している庭ですね。

白幡●谷さんが指摘されたように、植治はクライアントの意見や要求をみごとに受け入れていますね。その軸になったのは植物と水の扱い方、もう一つは永田さんがおっしゃった絵画性。一本の木、一つの滝を描くのではなく、それをとおして自然の総合性、全体性を描こうとしたのが植治。そこに植治の非凡な才能があったように思います。

一方の重森三玲は、巨石と石組み。石が立っていて、石のほうから迫ってくる。植治も石をじょうずに使うが、植治の石組みは一歩引いてくれる。

笹岡●ただ、二人とも平安・鎌倉期の『作庭記』以降の決まりごとのようなものは忠実に守る——そういった流れを踏まえている点では共通しますね。

いけばなの世界でも決まりごとがあります。禁忌と申しますが、してはいけない決まりごと、つまりタブーです。未生流の始祖である未生斎一甫は江戸時代の人ですが、彼の口述したいけばなの伝書『挿花百練』には、「三十六ヶ条禁忌」というものが載っています。禁忌というとわずらわしい印象をもたれるかもしれませんが、禁忌というのは先人が築いた優れた手法でもあるんですね。たとえば、枝と枝とが交差している状態は「見切り」という禁忌です。けんかしているように見えて非礼なので取り除くのです。

もちろん、禁忌は絶対のものではなく、わざとその基本を破ることもあります。型と同じようなものかもしれません。型破りはよいけれど、型無しではおもしろくない。型があるから、型を踏まえているからこそ、自由な表現ができるのです。

谷●先だって亡くなられた中村宗哲さんが、同じ趣旨のことを言っておられましたね。宗哲さんのお家は、茶の湯道具の「千家十職」のなかでも漆器がご専門ですが、そこには型があるわけです。利休型なら利休型。はたから見ると、そういう型に押し込められて窮屈ではないかと見られるが、じつはその型があることによって創造性が生まれるとおっしゃる。

魔法に満ちた日本の庭

永田●私は仕事でフランスに行っていて、久しぶりに京都に戻ってきたのですが、無鄰菴に一歩足を踏み入れたとたんに、「これぞ日本」と思いましたね。風も木も空もヨーロッパとはぜんぜん違う。

私は絵描きですので、尊敬する画家はたくさんいますが、もっともお手本とするのは、じつは自然。先ほど、この庭の奥まで歩いたんですが、私の頭の中に「これは人工の自然だ」という意識はあっても、滝の手前にある沢飛石*の中央

●TANI: Of course, he must have had a deep knowledge of tea ceremony. This is why he could understand Tokuan's vision. If he hadn't known anything about tea ceremony or Noh Theater, he would have never been able to realize this garden.

●SHIRAHATA: In short, Tokuan had the idea of creating a pond garden where a boat could float and Ueji realized it.

●TANI: Another peculiarity of this garden is that there is a stage for traditional Japanese dance extending over the pond.

●SHIRAHATA: I don't think there is any other garden where it is possible to perform tea ceremony on a boat.

●TANI: Yes, I think this is the only place where it is possible.

Creativity and Self-Assertion

●SASAOKA: The two famous landscape designers, Ueji and SHIGEMORI Mirei, even if they lived at different times, are very often compared to each other; the audacity of SHIGEMORI Mirei and the delicacy of Ueji. The difference between these two men could be seen as the difference between rocks and plants.

●NAGATA: I love the gardens by SHIGEMORI Mirei. They were not created to receive visitors gently; they are pure design.

●SHIRAHATA: As Mr. TANI said, Ueji's creations reflect the demands and the ideas of his clients. Water and plants are the principal elements in his gardens. Another thing is the framing, as Ms. NAGATA said. Ueji was not thinking of just one tree or one waterfall, he was thinking about the garden as a single unified whole. I think this is Ueji's extraordinary talent.

On the other hand, SHIGEMORI Mirei's creations are characterized by huge rocks and powerful stone arrangements. Mirei's stones are standing. They press down on the visitor. Ueji also had a skilful way with rocks, but his stone arrangements are lying down, they are more reserved.

●SASAOKA: But both Ueji and Mirei respected the traditional rules set by the "sakutei-ki," the oldest book about gardening in Japan. In this sense, they are in the same lineage.

In ikebana, there are also rules. There are things that cannot be done, taboos. When you talk about taboos, they usually sound burdensome, but actually they are the essence of our ancestors' technique. For example, crossing branches is a taboo.

立って滝を見ると、苔むした大きな岩に私は深山の気配を感じました。

その同じ石の上で振り返りますと、水音をたてて流れている水が、ほんの数メートル先ではさざ波一つたてない静かな空間になっている。ほんとうに不思議に思えてしようがないんです。このわずかの空間に深山から、平野から、もしかすると大海にまでつながる世界を表現している。それを計算して大きな自然観をここにまとめる力というのはすごいなと。

いまさらながら、日本の庭は魔法に満ちているなと思いますね。植治は、こういう空間をあやつる魔術師のような不思議な力をもった人ですね。

笹岡●水と樹と石をやさしく調和させることで、一つの小宇宙を具現化した庭ですね。しかも、華やかな世界。

永田●建物だけあっても少しも美しくなくて、周りに庭があってこそ美しい。私はそういうものに暮らしの風景を感じます。小さな家が一軒あって、そこに里山が拡がっている、そういう景観が都市の真ん中にいまもあることの不思議さ。京都の文化のすごさだなって思います。

谷●一口で言うと「市中の山居」。人が山の中に行くのではなくて、町なかに山のありさまをつくるという趣向です。

茶の湯は、連歌や和歌の影響を強く受けますが、連歌や和歌数寄の考え方は隠遁あるいは閑居するという要素を強く要求した。脱俗して山の中で小さな庵をむすび、そこで歌づくりにはげむ、そういう考え方が強かった。しかし、茶の湯は山の中に行かなくてよい、さらに言えば脱俗しなくても、入道しなくてもよい。いまの暮らしのなかに、かつての歌詠みの人たちが営んだような庵とその風景を

雁掛けの飛び石〈何有荘〉

Stepping stones snaking through the moss in Kaiu-sō

It looks like if they are fighting together so we take them out.

Of course, those taboos are not absolute and it can happen that we break them intentionally. Art that breaks through the forms is interesting, but something that is without form is not. It's because you are based in the form that you can express yourself freely.

● *TANI*: An artisan who made tools for tea ceremony used to say the same. For lacquered ware there are definite models. Looking from outside it seems to be very narrow and conservative, but the artisan used to say that it was because there were those models that creativity arose.

The Magic of Japanese Gardens

● *NAGATA*: I was in France for work and I hadn't been back to Kyoto for a while. When I stepped into Murin-an, I thought: "this is Japan." The trees, the wind, the sky, everything is different from Europe.

I am an illustrator and there are many painters whom I respect, but the model I prefer is still nature. When I arrived, I walked up to the end of the garden. Even though I had in mind that this space was artificial, when I stood on the stepping stones in front of the mossy waterfall, I felt as though I were deep in the mountains. I turned back, and the same water that was falling loudly from the waterfall was now flowing smoothly in a quiet pond without ripples. It was really marvelous. In such a small space the feel of a mountain valley, of a gentle field and of the wide sea had been recreated. It's impressive to see how Nature can be conveyed in a man-made garden.

I think that Japanese gardens are full of magic, and Ueji was a master magician who had this mysterious power to manipulate the elements.

● *SASAOKA*: By creating harmony between water, trees and rocks, Ueji created a microcosm.

● *NAGATA*: A building on its own is nothing special; a villa is beautiful because it is surrounded by a garden. In Murin-an, I feel as though I were on

植治が好んだ糸落ちの滝〈何有荘〉
The upper part of the waterfall in Kaiu-sō

園遊会が日本の庭を変える

白幡●そういう茶の湯が、明治期に財界人を中心に活気を呈しますね。ブルジョワのお茶というか、新しい茶と茶会がはじまる。明治維新後の財界人には近代化、西洋化が必要だったが、その反面で日本的な茶を取り入れる。これはどうつながるのでしょうか。

谷●茶の湯の庭は「露地」*といい、かつては狭い空間でした。植治の庭のような池泉廻遊式*の広い庭とは基本的に異なるものだった。だから、東山山麓に別荘を営んだ数寄者たちは、かつての露地・茶庭*をここに展開してはだめだ、この条件を活かして庭をつくるべきだと思ったん

でしょうね。そこで、池を穿ち、その池を廻る池庭の構成を考える。だから、茶庭というのは「似非自然」かもしれませんが、自然をたいせつにするし、日本人の基本的な考え方の一つに自然との共生がある。自然をいじって人間に都合のよいように変えるとか対峙するのではなくて、人間も自然とともに暮らそうと。

永田さんが、「庭の奥に行ってみると山里のような風情があった」とおっしゃいました。まさしくそういうものを、庭園の全体にではなく局面、局面に配し、そのうえで全体として新しい庭園をつくろうと考えたように思うのですがね。

白幡●植治が東山を遠望する地形をうまく使った借景と、開放感のある広びろとした芝生をお茶の席に取り入れたのは、茶の湯にとっては新しい経験でしょうか。

谷●異質とまではいかないのですが、明治になるまでの茶の湯はせいぜい4、5人まで。それが大人数を招く茶になると、二畳敷き、三畳敷きの茶室と狭い露地では

谷 晃 たに・あきら
1944年、愛知県に生まれる。京都大学史学科卒業。芸術学博士。神戸市にある香雪美術館勤務をへて、88年から野村美術館学芸部長。専攻は茶の湯文化史。茶の湯に関わる広い分野で深く幅広い知見に定評がある。歴史や文化の机上の研究だけでなく、点前、料理なども実践的にたしなむ。著書に『茶会記の風景』、『わかりやすい茶の湯の文化』、『茶人たちの日本文化史』などがある。

TANI Akira
Born in 1944, in Aichi prefecture. Graduated from the department of History of Kyoto University. Doctor of Fine Arts. In 1988 he became the Curator of the Nomura Art Museum. He is also director of the Tea Ceremony Institute of Japan.

a little farm in the countryside. It's amazing to imagine that this space is in the middle of a city. I think this is the marvel of Japanese culture.

●TANI: In one word, this is called a "mountain hermitage in the middle of the city." It's the idea that people are not going to withdraw to the mountains, but recreate the way things are in the mountains in their villas in the city.

Tea ceremony was heavily influenced by *renga* and *tanka*, two different forms of traditional Japanese poetry that yearned for life in a quiet retreat. To rise above worldly concerns and to live in a little retreat in the mountains was the ideal of Japanese poetry. But in tea ceremony, there is no need to go into the mountains, no need to be detached from worldly matters. You can recreate the scenery of the ancient poets' retreats in this life. I think this is the spirit of the way of tea.

Garden Parties that Revolutionized Japanese Gardens

●SHIRAHATA: Tea ceremony during the Meiji era was mostly an activity for businessmen. I may say the tea ceremony of the "bourgeoisie." It was the beginning of a new way of tea. After the Meiji Restoration, businessmen started on a course towards westernization and modernization on the one side, but on the other side they adopted tea ceremony. Why did they adopt those two opposite ideas?

●TANI: The traditional gardens for tea ceremony were very narrow places, fundamentally different from the wide and bright gardens by Ueji. All the businessmen who created their villas at the bottom of the Higashiyama hills tried to adapt their gardens to the natural conditions of the location: they created pond gardens.

Japanese gardens are artificial representations of nature but still, the basis of Japanese philosophy is a symbiotic relationship with nature. Japanese do not tamper with nature, they live together with it.

Ms. NAGATA said that the Murin-an garden was like a rural scene. Undoubtedly it is. Each part of this garden recreates an image from nature. This is the prototype of the modern Japanese garden.

●SHIRAHATA: The fact that Ueji borrowed the Higashiyama hills as background scenery and created wide-open spaces with lawns for tea gardens, was it something new in the world of tea ceremony?

●TANI: I would not say that it was totally different. Before the Meiji Restoration, a tea ceremony

対応できない。それで芝生を植えて廻遊できるように考えたと思います。
永田●サロンの色あいが濃くなったんでしょうか。密談がそこで行なわれたり、縁談がまとまったりと……。(笑)
谷●西洋の影響もあってパーティという感覚だったと思いますね。
白幡●皇室が新宿御苑で開く園遊会は、日本の宴会と西洋のパーティの要素を取りこんでできたように思いますが。
永田●西洋の習慣にならって女性がご主人と一緒に正装して出かける機会が増えると、お庭での催しは気に入っているお召し物を上から下まで見せるいい機会になったと思いますね。
谷●碧雲荘にはきれいどころがたくさん来ている写真が残っています。そういう女性にずいぶん喜ばれたんでしょうね。
永田●着物は、肩から裾まで同じ色彩、同じ世界を表現していて、そういう女性の着物姿を美しく見せる空間が日本の庭。ことに、水辺があり、広いお庭に緑の木立があるお庭だと着物の色彩が映えるんです。晴れやかな空間ですから、きれいどころの方がたも、やっぱり力が入ったと思います。(笑)
谷●一世一代のおめかしをしてね。(笑)

自然を演出するという思想

白幡●植治は、「幽邃というものを考えている」という言葉を残しています。幽邃とは本来、比較的閉ざされた落ち着きのある庭にあてはまる表現ですが、「自分はもう少し広いものを考えている。これからは岡山の後楽園みたいな庭もだいじだ」と。後楽園のような広びろとした大名庭にならって、茶の湯の庭に少し広めの芝生の空間を入れたり、遠くを覗けるようにしたのは植治のアイデアだったのでしょうか。それとも、茶会に新しい要素を入れようとした明治の茶人たちの考えだったのでしょうか。
谷●芝生を入れた茶庭は、植治の庭がきっかけかどうかはわかりませんが、明治以降の産物であることは間違いない。得庵も芝生を意識していて、そこそこの広さの芝生を確保しています。

木の間がくれに風景を楽しむという趣向は江戸時代の初めからあって、茶人の古田織部に「海少しある木の間かな」という言葉があるんです。木立のあいだから海が少し見えるのが茶庭にはいいんだ、オープンに見せるのも隠してしまうのもだめだと。だから、無鄰庵のように全体を借景として取り込んだ茶庭はない。

ただ、小堀遠州がつくった岡山県高梁市の頼久寺の庭は明らかに川向こうの山を借景に取り入れていて、借景という考え方自体がなかったわけではない。しかし、木立で覆って、ある種の閉鎖空間をつくる気持ちのほうが強かった気がします。
永田●池とか水の流れは……。
谷●水は取り入れる場合があります。やはり江戸前期の茶人の金森宗和は、「水を少しだけ流して、あとは細かい石を敷き詰めて、かつて滝があった風情を演出した」というように書いています。ただ、それはわざとらしいという批判を受けるんです。あまりにもつくりすぎる、作為が目だつと。じっさいには手を加えるんですが、見た目に作為を感じさせないのがいいんだという考え方です。

was for four or five persons at most. After the Meiji Restoration, it became common to invite large numbers of people and it was impossible to fit so many persons in the traditional narrow gardens and small tearooms. I believe this is why they thought about planting lawns.
●*NAGATA*: May I say that it became much more like a "salon," or a reception for confidential conversation (laughs).
●*TANI*: With the influence from the West, it was the beginning of "garden parties" too.
●*SHIRAHATA*: I think that the receptions held by the Emperor in Tokyo were the first that mixed a traditional Japanese banquet with a "garden party."
●*NAGATA*: Learning from the West, the number of occasions on which ladies were able to go out with their husbands increased. Walking in the gardens was a good opportunity for them to show off all their finery.
●*TANI*: There are many pictures remaining of those women in the garden of Hekiun-sō. They must have enjoyed it very much.
●*NAGATA*: Modern Japanese gardens are the best place to demonstrate the beauty of kimonos that are made in one piece from the shoulders to the hem. The nuances of kimono colors reflect particularly well in the water and in the bright spaces of the modern Japanese garden. I think that all those ladies displayed themselves proudly in the gardens (laughs).
●*TANI*: They must have specially dressed up for the occasion (laughs).

Creating Nature
●*SHIRAHATA*: Ueji said that it was important to keep in mind the image of a deep mountain valley when you created a garden. That is, a dense and serene garden. But he said that he also thought of wide-open spaces, like the gardens of the feudal lords. But was it in fact Ueji's idea to introduce lawns in tea gardens, or was it an idea from the tea masters of the Meiji era?
●*TANI*: I don't know if Ueji's gardens were the first where lawns were introduced, but there is no doubt that they were a product of the Meiji era. Tokuan, the owner of the Hekiun-sō garden, was very conscious of the need for a lawn and there is quite a large lawn space in the garden.
F URATA Oribe, one of the great tea masters of the Edo period said that in a tea garden, it was neither good to create a panoramic view of the sea,

永田●京都の庭は、劇場の舞台のようにだれが見ても美しいものを、無駄を排して必要なものを必要な場所に置いてつくられるものですね。いっぽうで、私が絵を描くときに向きあう自然は、その元になった自然。つくられた世界をそのまま描こうという気にはならなくても、気持ちの安らぎとか与えられるインスピレーションは、庭のほうがすごく強い。

白幡●それが生の自然と庭との違いということでしょうね。

永田●アーティストの作品を模写してもしようがない。(笑)まして、空や風、この植物の香りまで含めてのアートです。これを鑑賞するには私たちがここを訪れるしかない。こういう空間を構築する力をもったアーティストを心から尊敬しますね。自分の表現の世界に力を与えてほしい、活かしてほしいと。

庭といけばなの深い関係

笹岡●いけばなも、庭と切り離して語ることはできません。中世、枯山水の庭ができたころに、いけばなは盛んになるんです。自然を写した写実的な庭園が多かったのが、室町期に枯山水が出てくると植栽が減ります。そう、緑が少なくなった。身近に植物を感じられなくなったことで、家の中で花を飾るいけばなが普及したのではないかと言われています。

　日本庭園の「天地人」の配置も、いけばなと共通します。石組みの配置もいけばなのデザインも、同じデザイン手法にもとづいているのです。

白幡●いけばなの天地人というのは……。

笹岡●江戸時代に生まれた「生花」という花の型があります。天地人という三つの位をもった3本の枝だけで構成されるシンプルないけばなです。太陽と地球があり、そのあいだにわれわれ人間がいる。花で、小宇宙を表現するのです。私はそこに日本人の花への思いが隠されていると思うんですね。未生斎一甫の伝書には、「花を生けるときに、目の前の花だけに執心してはいけない」と書かれています。花を生けるときは、「花の生い立ちにまで思いを馳せなさい」と。

永田●すばらしい言葉ですね。

笹岡●太陽がなかったら植物は光合成ができないし、大地がなかったら水や養分を吸い上げられない。そういった天地の恵みを凝縮させたのが花であると。

永田●象徴ですものね。

笹岡●私たちは花を美しく見せることばかりに心をとめるのではなく、天地の恵みである花を通じて、天地を含む宇宙全体のことを考えなくてはいけない。私たちは、花を生けることによって、人として

笹岡隆甫　ささおか・りゅうほ
1974年、当代家元・勲甫氏の孫として京都に生まれる。3歳から家元の手ほどきを受ける。京都大学工学部建築学科卒業。京都大学大学院博士後期課程を中退し、2000年から華道に専念。国の内外で「いけばなパフォーマンス」を展開する。狂言師・茂山千作氏と「花狂言」を共演するなど、異分野とのコラボレーションにも積極的に取り組む。著書に『美的生活のヒント』がある。

SASAOKA Ryūho
Born in 1974, in Kyoto. He is a direct line descendant of the Sasaoka school of ikebana. He studied ikebana from the age of three. Graduated from Kyoto University. Master of Architecture. He dropped out of his Masters course and devoted himself to ikebana, Japanese flower arrangement.

nor to hide it completely. Good taste was to show it in the distance through the trees. This is why, up to the Meiji era, there were no tea gardens like the one at Murin-an, where the entire range of hills are borrowed as background scenery. It does not mean that the concept of borrowing the background scenery was absent from tea gardens but I think that the idea of enclosed spaces was stronger.
●*NAGATA*: what about ponds and streams?
●*TANI*: In the past there were already tea gardens with water features. The tea master KANAMORI Sōwa said that he created a very fine stream and that he placed in it little rocks at random to recreate the feel of a waterfall. However, he was criticized because it was too studied and unnatural. All gardens are man-made but it's good not to show artifice. This was the way of thinking at that time.
●*NAGATA*: A Japanese garden is like theatrical scenery, every element has its place and there are no useless objects, so that anyone who looks at it will find it beautiful. When I'm painting I do not try to paint things as I see them. The peaceful feeling that one can find in a garden is a great source of inspiration for me.
●*SHIRAHATA*: Is this the difference between Nature and gardens?
●*NAGATA*: It's no use to just copy someone's work of art. I think that the sky, the wind, the scent of plants, they are all art. To appreciate this, you have to actually visit the place yourself. I deeply respect the artists who can create spaces where you can have such an experience.

Gardens and Ikebana
●*SASAOKA*: I think that there is a very close relationship between gardens and ikebana. During the Muromachi Period (1336-1573), ikebana flourished when the dry gardens appeared. In the dry landscapes, there are fewer plants. It is said that because there was less green in the gardens, people started to decorate the interior with flowers.
　There is also the technique of "*Tenchijin*," the "heaven, earth and human" that is common to both ikebana and gardening.
●*SHIRAHATA*: What is that technique precisely?
●*SASAOKA*: The technique of "heaven, earth and human" is to symbolize a microcosm with only three branches. It forms a triangle. There is the sun, the earth and in the middle, the human. I think that in this technique is hidden the spirit of the Japanese art of flower arrangement. It is said

のあり方や美しい生き方のヒントを花から学びます。生花を構成する天地人には、そういう想いが託されています。

永田●いいお話ですね。これからそう思ってお花を見ます。（笑）

白幡●私は、立花と立石には共通するところがあって、いけばなは石の組み方から出てきたと考えています。しかも、庭の植物が減ったことで花が興ったという笹岡さんの指摘はたいへん興味深いお話です。すると、明治期になると庭と同様、なにか新しい現象が……。

笹岡●明治は、海外から新しい植物が入ってきた時代です。西洋種のユリとかバラとか、まっすぐで大きな花に当時の華道家たちはいろいろ苦心していますが、そういった頭が大きくて重たいものを生けるために剣山が開発されて、「投入」や「盛花」という新しい花のかたちが生み出されたのがこの時代です。

しかし、かつてあったものを捨て去ってはいない。室町時代の立花も江戸時代の生花も残り、明治の投入、盛花が加わる。積み上げられているんです。

谷●茶の湯でも同じですね。従来の少人数の茶は、やはり基本として存続する。だけれど、現実はそれに対応できないから、こういう広いところでやる茶が主流になったわけです。かつての技法やスタイルを否定しないことでは同じですね。

苔に落ちた赤いツバキの花は美しい

永田●京都で暮らしていても、私はとくに日本画的な構図の取り方とか、日本画的な画材を使おうという意識はまったくなかったのですが、こんどのフランスでの展覧会では、染料で絹に描いた絵を持って行ったんです。日本のみなさんからも「日本画みたいですね」って言われるし、フランスの方は「日本の心を感じる」と言ってくださった。私にも日本画から受け継がれる日本人の絵画の美意識がDNAとして厳然としてあるのかなと思ったのですが、とにかく日本画の方は余白の使い方がおじょうずでしょう。揺るぎのない位置になにかを一点置いたり、省略したりと。それはお庭をつくる感覚にも近いと思うのですよ。

私は四季をテーマに描いたのですが、その一枚に私の大好きなツバキが苔の上に落ちた早春の風景を描いたんです。緑の苔に真っ赤なツバキが落ちている。それを見たフランス人が、「なぜ落ちているものを描くのか、死んだ花はゴミみたいなものだ」と。しかし、「落ちたツバキもたしかに美しい。これまでこんな視点で見たことがなかった」と。

笹岡●フラワー・アレンジメントには最高の瞬間というのがあります。結婚式の飾花なら、そのパーティの時間にベストの状態になるよう、盛りを迎えた花を多く使う。でも、いけばなには最高の瞬間がないんです。つぼみで生けて、そのつぼみが徐々にほころび、満開を迎え、やがて凋落を迎える。その命の移ろいのすべてを見届けるのがいけばな。命に軽重はありません。赤ちゃんの命もお年寄りの命も同じようにかけがえのないもの。いけばなで表現するのは命そのもの。

永田●もっと長いわけですね。

笹岡●命の最期まで見届けることがだいじ。

that you should not give too much attention to the flower that is in front of your eyes. When you arrange flowers, you have to understand the feelings of each flower.
●*NAGATA*: That is a nice phrase.
●*SASAOKA*: Without the sun, there would be no photosynthesis, without the earth, plants would not be able to draw up the sap. Flowers are the condensation of the grace of the Universe.
●*NAGATA*: The flower is the symbol of grace, for sure.
●*SASAOKA*: This is why we have to think of the whole universe when we arrange flowers. It's not a matter of just showing the beauty of the flowers; arranging one flower is to think about the grace of the universe. We learn about humankind from flowers.
●*NAGATA*: That is a nice way of thinking. From now on I will try to see flowers in this way (laughs).
●*SHIRAHATA*: My point of view is that there is a common trait between raising stones and arranging flowers. I think that ikebana comes from stone settings. Moreover, Mr. SASAOKA's comment, that during the Muromachi period, when plants decreased in the gardens, flower arrangement flourished, was very interesting. So in the Meiji era, as with the gardens, did a new form of ikebana arise?
●*SASAOKA*: The Meiji era was the period when new flowers began to come in from overseas: the lily or the rose from the Western countries, etc. New techniques appeared for arranging those straight stalks with large, heavy flowers at the top. But it doesn't mean that they threw away the ancient techniques. In each period, new techniques arose and they built on the others.
●*TANI*: It's the same in tea ceremony. The traditional tea ceremony with only a few guests endures as the basic pattern. But because it didn't fit with reality, tea ceremony with large numbers of people became the mainstream. It's not a denial of the traditional techniques and styles.

The Beauty of a Fallen Camellia Flower
●*NAGATA*: Even though I live in Kyoto, I had never consciously used the compositions or subjects of traditional Japanese paintings. But lately, I held an exhibition in France and I took a picture that I had painted on silk. Japanese people told me that it looked like a traditional Japanese painting and French people told me that they could feel the Japanese spirit in this painting. I painted a fallen camellia, a flower that I particularly like. A red

落ちたツバキまで見届けるからこそ日本人は命の尊さを感じとり、枯れゆくのがかわいそう、散りゆくのは忍びないという、いたわりや思いやりの気持ちを育む。その花が「少しでも長く元気でいるように」と水を換えたり、足下を焼いたりと、いろいろな「養い」を施す。

谷●茶庭の掃除にしても、落ち葉一つないのが美しいのではなくて、落ち葉の二つ三つ落ちているぐらいがいい。(笑)

永田●西洋人には理解されない、すばらしい美意識ですよね。

庭は変化を容認するアート

白幡●庭にも、最高の瞬間は決まっていないですね。そもそも庭には完成ということがない。どういう扱いをするかで、良くもなれば悪くもなる。時間を内包するのが日本の庭です。だから、だれの作かも、はっきりしなくなる。植治がつくったといっても、ずいぶん変わる。

無鄰庵の庭が100年以上もっているのは、その後を維持管理する人たちの技術や感性が優れているということですね。

永田●最初のプランが受け継がれているわけではないのですか。

白幡●日本の庭には設計図がないんです。平面図も立面図もない。その場で、自分の感性のもとにデザインする。

永田●頭のなかに設計図があっても、変更は可能なんですね、おそらく。運ばれてきた石にしたって、木の枝ぶりにしたって、最初のイメージどおりであるわけがないですものね。柔軟なゆとりをもちながら、全体をゆるぎのないものにするというのはすばらしいですね。

白幡先生がおっしゃったように、ほとんどの芸術はつくられた時点から劣化に向かって進むのは宿命です。ところが、植治の庭に不可欠な植物は毎年成長する。すると、庭は変化を容認するアート。しかも大きく、よりよく変化する可能性をもった作品ですね。

白幡●苔むす石にしても、その苔を残すかどうかは、その時代の美意識などを総合した結果。笹岡さんは先ほど、「いけばなは時間を生けている」と表現されましたが、なるほどそうですね。いけばなはやっぱり、庭と心が似ている。

笹岡●ええ、時間経過がだいじです。

様式美がつくる日本の美の伝統

白幡●植治は、明治という新しい時代の雰囲気のなかで、無鄰庵という日本庭園をつくった。古い日本の庭を再現するのではなく、新しい時代の息吹を受け入れている。いけばなもまた、先人が残したものをプラスして捉えるなど、伝統をだいじにしている。しかし、近代という違

永田 萌 ながた・もえ
1949年、兵庫県に生まれる。「カラーインクの魔術師」とよばれる類まれな色彩感覚と、花と妖精をテーマにした夢あふれる作風で、画業30年を得たいまも第一線で活躍する。1987年に『花待洋月に』で、ボローニャ国際児童図書展グラフィック賞を受賞。絵本、画集、エッセイなどこれまでに130冊余りを出版。近著に『ふりむけば花の香り』。京都で「ギャラリー妖精村」を主宰する。

NAGATA Moe
Born in Hyogo Prefecture. Illustrator, painter for illustrated books and also author of essays. She paints the world of fairies using the particularly light and velvety effect of watercolors ink. She has published more than 100 books.

camellia flower was lying on green moss. The French persons who saw it told me that to see beauty in a flower that had fallen was something completely new for them.

●*SASAOKA*: This is the difference between ikebana and flower arrangement. When you decorate a room for a party, you choose the flowers that will be in bloom, in the best shape for the duration of the party. But in ikebana, there is not only one best moment. You arrange the flowers coming into bud, then the buds blossom, wither and fall. To watch the flower to its end is the spirit of ikebana. Ikebana expresses the whole cycle of life.

●*NAGATA*: This is a long cycle.

●*SASAOKA*: It's important to watch the flower to its end. It is because you look at the camellia to its end that you can feel the preciousness of life. You wish that the flower will last as long as possible, so you give it water, you give it attention.

●*TANI*: When we clean the tea gardens too, it's not considered beautiful to sweep up all the fallen flowers, it's good taste to leave one or two flowers behind (laughs).

●*NAGATA*: It's a very refined aesthetic.

Gardens are an Art that Allows Change

●*SHIRAHATA*: It is the same for gardens; there is no best moment. There is no completion for a garden. According to the attention you give to the garden, it can become better, but also worse. Japanese gardens change with time. This is why people forget who's work it was. With the passing of time, gardens change a lot.

The fact that one hundred years later, Ueji's gardens still endure is thanks to the maintenance and the excellent skill and aesthetic sense of the gardeners.

●*NAGATA*: Does it mean that the gardeners do not respect the original plan?

●*SHIRAHATA*: There are no plans for Japanese gardens. Gardeners follow their instincts on the site.

●*NAGATA*: So it means that even if they have the plan already complete in their minds, it is still possible to make changes. It is true that the form of the rocks and trees that have been brought may not be exactly as expected. In a sense, gardeners are very flexible but the gardens they create are very strong. It's marvelous.

Mr. SHIRAHATA said that almost all works of art decline after they have been created. However, the plants in Ueji's gardens are always growing. It means that gardens are an art that allows changes.

う原理も持ち込むので、それを引き受けながら発展させようとすると、たいへん苦労することになると思うのですがね。

笹岡●私自身は、禁忌があるから苦労するということはないですね。伝統の花を生ける場合、禁忌は守るべき絶対的なものです。けれども、花は時代とともに変わり、積み上げられるものでもあります。

新しい花は戦後にも生まれましたが、そこでは従来の型を否定するような花が生み出されました。たとえば、三角形の型に花を収めるとだれが生けても宗匠の花が生けられる、きれいな花が生けられるという優れた方法論があります。これにたいし、「三角形はもう古い、新しいことをしましょう」と、これまでの型をアンチテーゼとする花を志向する時代がくる。すると、禁忌は意味をなさなくなり、自然を写すことも意味をなさなくなる。いけばなをアートとして捉える時代になるんですね。これは全国的な流れになりました。西洋の抽象画の手法を取り入れ、それまで日本的な美として志向していたアシンメトリーの、左右非対称の美を捨て、カンディンスキーの絵画に見られるような左右対称を基本としたデザインが生み出されました。

白幡●西洋とはまた違うものでしたね。

笹岡●いけばなの伝統的手法は否定するが、日本人のDNAのようなものは残したという感じはありますね。建築でも庭園でもいけばなでも、アシンメトリーを日本人はだいじにしてきましたから。

白幡●それは伝統の継承なのでしょうか。それとも、まったく新しいこと……。

笹岡●基本的には、継承していません。その時代、初めて古典を継承しない型が生み出されたんです。西洋の抽象画の影響が大きかったんでしょうね。

しかし、これまでの花が完全に捨て去られたわけではありません。これまでどおり、古典花も生けていますし、戦後の現代花も完全なシンメトリーではなく、アシンメトリーの要素を含んでいる。

私は個人的には古典花のほうが好きです。落ち着くというか、不安定な美のほうが日本人にはしっくりきますね。

白幡●伝統の継承は、芸術をつくるときの源泉としてはたいへん役にたつという以上に、なくてはならないものですね。

笹岡●芸術というとどうなのかわかりません……。私は、いけばなはアートではないと思っています。花で自分自身を表現するのがいけばなではありません。われわれは黒衣の役割を果たしているのであって、だいじなのは、花のよさを引き立たせること。それがわれわれ華道家の仕事です。自分を表現する表現者ではない。ここは微妙なところですが、私自身はアーティストではないと考えています。

永田●笹岡さんがそれを言い切ると、なにか清々しく見える。（笑）

自己主張しないという美意識

白幡●谷さんは先ほど、碧雲荘は植治の庭とはちょっと違うんだというニュアンスをおっしゃった。つまり、いけばなでは花を生かすのが基本であると同様に、植治は自分を抑えて、木と水を生かす、自然を生かす、クライアントの想いを生かすなど、ほかのものを活かそうとしていたんじゃないかということですね。

On top of that, they are works that can grow better and better.

●*SHIRAHATA*: Look at the rocks that were over grown by moss. Should we remove it or let it grow? The choice will reflect the aesthetic sense of the time. Mr. SASAOKA said that the art of ikebana was to appreciate the flower's growth. It is true that the spirit of ikebana is close to that of gardening.

●*SASAOKA*: For sure, the process of time is very important.

An Aesthethic that is not Self-Asserting

●*SHIRAHATA*: Ueji created gardens in the mood of the Meiji period. Especially in this Murin-an garden he did not try to copy the ancient Japanese gardens; he introduced the new trend of his time. In ikebana too, you integrate new things without losing the traditions. During the Meiji period new principles were introduced from the West, and Japanese people had to accept their traditional culture but also allow it to evolve. I think they had a hard time.

●*SASAOKA*: For me, it is not a hardship to have rules. When I arrange flowers in a traditional way, I respect the rules. But, ikebana changes with the times. The Meiji period was not the only turning point in ikebana, the post-war period was another one.

For example, if you respect the traditional "*Tenchijin*" technique of "heaven, earth and human," anyone can arrange flowers beautifully. This is a central principle, but post-war, people wanted to do something new so they worked on the antithesis of this rule. Then the traditional rules had no more meaning, including the reproduction of nature. It was a period when everything had to be original. Ikebana was also influenced by western abstract paintings. The Japanese traditional aesthetic is based on asymmetry, but at that time a symmetric ikebana developed, like the paintings by Kandinski.

●*SHIRAHATA*: But still, it was different from western art.

●*SASAOKA*: We say "Western art" but personally I don't think that ikebana is an art. In ikebana, the will of the creator is not that important. We are like the people working behind the stage; our work is to show flowers to their advantage. In this sense, we are not expressing ourselves. This is a delicate point but I don't think of myself as an artist.

●*NAGATA*: When Mr. SASAOKA puts it like that,

谷●職人というのは、どんなジャンルでも同じだろうと思いますが、日本では自己主張するとかえってだめですね。おっしゃるように使うもの、あるいは対象ですね、建築なら木材の性質を一本一本見きわめて、それをうまく組み合わせるのが本来の職人じゃないでしょうか。クライアントの意向を踏まえるとはいえ、施主自身は作品をつくれない。つくるのはあくまで職人でありアーティスト。

笹岡●個性というのは、自分を消して消して、それでも残るものだろうと。私も、花のよさを引き立たせよう、引き立たせようと願って生けます。それでも私の作品と祖父の作品とでは、なにかが違う。自分を消しても消しきれなかったもの、そこで残ったのがほんとうの個性なのでしょう。クライアントの意見を聞き、自然の植栽を活かして、自分は一歩引いて表現する。それでも残ったのが植治の個性ではないかと……。

永田●私の仕事はイラストレーターで、画家と大きく違うのは、依頼を受けて制作する点。どこかの企業が、私の描くバラの絵を使って新しい商品をつくりたいという依頼があって初めて成立する仕事です。作庭家も、まず依頼する人ありき。植治がどんなにすばらしいプランをもっていても、それを求めてくれる人がいてくれないと、視覚化できないわけですよね。どこか共通点がある気がします。

白幡●植治には、水の魔術師であり、水の絵師のようなところがあった。水をとてもじょうずに使った。しかし、どんな材料を使うにしても、この庭にどういう要望が寄せられているかが元になっている。

永田●じつは、私も厳密に言うとアーティストではないと思っています。求めに応えて愛されるものをつくるプロの絵描きだからです。ですから、相手の想いをじっくり聴いて、その人の意向に添うことをたいせつにします。それをしたからといって、私の描いた絵がほかの人の絵になることはない。私はそう信じていますから、引けるかぎりは引きます。

でも、譲れないところはあります。植治にしても、「これをやったら自分じゃない」というものはきちっとおもちだったと思います。他人が頭に描く以上のものを見せてあげるのが快感ですからね。

白幡●谷さんは、野村徳七と白楊あるいは植治との関係において、碧雲荘の庭を、どうとらえていらっしゃいますか。

植治に特徴的な技法が読みとれる
無鄰庵の瓢箪池とその周辺

The pond at the end of the Murin-an garden creates a peaceful atmosphere

it sounds very noble (laughs).

●SHIRAHATA: Mr. TANI said that the garden of Hekiun-sō was a bit different from Ueji's other gardens. As in ikebana, where what is most important is to show the flowers to their advantage, maybe Ueji held back his self-assertion and tried show the trees, and the water to their advantage while also taking into account the intentions of his clients.

●TANI: I think that Japanese artisans, whatever their field, do not show too much self-assertion. As you said, they have to find the best materials and the best tools to bring them together. They have to take into account the intentions of the client, but a client could not produce the work on his own, so in the end, the result is the work of the artisan.

●SASAOKA: I think that an artisan holds back his individuality, but even so, there is something that remains. When I arrange flowers I always think of

谷●野村得庵があの空間において日本文化を彼なりに理解して再構築しようとした場であるところに、碧雲荘の最大の特徴があります。その実現を手伝ったのが植治父子。ただ、得庵没後、得庵の意向に添った利用がされているかというと、かならずしもそうではない。

永田●しかし、図面がないのが庭だとしたら、それもいいのかもしれませんね。

白幡●庭をはじめ、日本の芸術に共通する一種の精神性というのは、「作品は私一人でつくったのではない、しかしその技には強い自負をしっかり込めている」というもの。

永田●そうです、それがすごいですね、まじめな民族だから。(笑)

谷●職人が似あっている。(笑)

精神性が潜んでこその日本の芸術

白幡●いけばなから見た日本の芸術の特性というのはどんなものでしょうか。

笹岡●いけばなにかぎらず、日本の芸術には共通する特性がたくさんありますね。不安定の美もあれば、余白の美や省略の美もあります。けれども、いちばん大きいのは、やはり想いじゃないかなと。

ペルーで花を生けたことがあるのですが、そのときに現地の方が、「日本のいけばなにはフィロソフィーがある」とおっしゃった。こちらが言葉で説明する前に、私の生けた花だけを見てそうおっしゃった。このとき、私が生けたのは、天地人を内包した「生花」。そうすると、いけばなというのは、人としてのあり方を学ぶところに本質があるのではないかと。

永田●それは茶の湯にも繋がるし、私たちのような新しいジャンルの仕事でも、そのことを心しないといけませんね。

笹岡●たんに美しく見せるだけではつまらないですからね。

永田●ほんとにそう。野に咲く一輪のほうが美しいといえば美しいですものね。命を借りて新しいものを表現しようとすれば、扱う人に精神の緊張が求められますよね。怖いことです。

笹岡●日本の庭には、そういったものがたくさん隠れている気がします。

近代の日本庭園の本質はどこに求められるか

白幡●日本の庭は、みなさんに浮き彫りにしていただいたように、完成時点がないから、現代の視点に合わせて使ってよい。おかしなところ、壊れたところは直してもよい。それは、植治にとってなんの障害でもなかった。そういうおおらかな造形からみても、この無鄰庵の庭は明治の庭の典型だと思います。

とはいえ、日本の庭園史を振り返ると、平安時代には寝殿造庭園*という代表的な様式があって、鎌倉・室町期には枯山水様式があり、江戸時代には廻遊式という様式があるが、明治以降にはまだ様式名がない。見る目が熟していないのか、独自の様式が表現できていないのか、明治以降の日本庭園の様式は尋ねられても、日本庭園という以外にない。

永田●それは思いがけないことですね。

白幡●しいていえば茶会式、園遊式。

谷●ある意味では、そうですね。

永田●じゃあ、そろそろ白幡先生が名付けないと……。(笑)

the best arrangement for the flowers I have at hand. However, my arrangements are very different from those of my grandfather. Maybe this difference could be called "individuality." Ueji took into account the intentions of his clients and tried to show the plants to their advantage but even so, Ueji's personal style remains.

●NAGATA: I am an illustrator; it means that I paint the requests of my clients. This is the difference from painters. For example, I receive the order to paint a red rose for a product and I paint a red rose. For gardeners, there is also an order. Even if you have marvelous plans in your head, if there is no one to order them, they will never be realized. This is why I think that artisans do not hold themselves back that much.

●SHIRAHATA: Ueji is said to have been a master magician with water. He used the water in his gardens very skillfully. But the bases of his creations were the orders and the materials he had available.

●NAGATA: To tell the truth, I don't think I'm an artist. I respond to an order and I try to paint something so that it will be appreciated. I listen carefully to the intentions of the client, and I try to handle it with great care. However, I believe that the painting I do is unique, it could not be painted by somebody else, so when I'm painting for someone, I try to respect his request as much as I can.

But there are some things that I cannot concede. I think that Ueji had this feeling too. It is a pleasant feeling to create something that surpasses the expectations of the client.

●SHIRAHATA: What does Mr. TANI think about the relationship between NOMURA Tokuan, the client, and Ueji and his son, the artisans, in the realization of the Hekiun-sō garden?

●TANI: NOMURA Tokuan tried to recreate a place for traditional Japanese culture and art; I think this is the principal distinguishing characteristic of the Hekiun-sō garden. Ueji and his son Hakuyō, they helped him to do it. But after Tokuan's death, the garden was not always used as planned.

●SHIRAHATA: I think that this spirit is common to gardening and to all the Japanese craft arts. A work of art is not the result of only one person, but the artisans are responding to a demand.

●NAGATA: This is marvelous for sure; the Japanese are very serious people (laughs).

●TANI: Japan is a nation of artisans (laughs).

白幡●植治がその代表ですが、近代日本の庭園は西洋、日本、いろいろな要素を混ぜ合わせ、融合させている。こういう様式をつくるには苦労したと思いますね。

谷●ひとつ思うのは、京都の庭というと、どちらかというと寺院に付属するものという意識が強かったですね。それを意図してか、意図せずしてか、寺院と完全に切り離した存在にしていることも、植治の特徴の一つかなという気もします。

白幡●疏水にそって財界人や政治家などの別荘に庭をつくることになった植治は、寺院と切り離された場に庭をつくる機会が与えられたという意味で、いい条件の一つになったかもしれません。植治自身が土地開発のディベロッパーのような役割を果たし、裕福な層に上質な住まい、庭園と宅地を提供した。奈良仏教は庭をつくらなかったが、平安仏教は庭をすごくだいじにした。京都の庭園の伝統は、基本的には仏教に関わる部分が大きくて、いまも京都の庭はお寺の庭に代表されますが、その京都の代表的な庭師である植治は、逆に宗教性とは距離をおいている。おもしろい現象です。

永田●意識して排除したんでしょうか。

白幡●いや、それはないと思いますよ。明治に至って社寺よりも世俗の経済力がぐっと上がって、宗教界をクライアントにする必要がなかったということ。もう一つは、岡崎の別荘地のディベロッパー的な仕事をしていたからでしょう。

笹岡●日本の建築自体、西洋の建築とくらべて庭との繋がりが深い。縁という灰色の空間があって、屋根の下にいながらにして屋外の四季のうつろいを感じること

The Modern Japanese Garden

●*SHIRAHATA*: When you look back on the history of Japanese gardens, one can realize that there is a style of garden for every period of history but not for the Meiji era. Is it because our eyes are not mature enough, or because there is no original style? When you ask about the style of the gardens in the Meiji period, the only answer is to talk about "Japanese gardens."

●*NAGATA*: This is unexpected.

●*SHIRAHATA*: We may talk about a "tea ceremony style" or a "garden party style."

●*TANI*: That's true, these could be good expressions.

●*NAGATA*: Now it is Mr. SHIRAHATA's job to find a name for this style (laughs).

●*SHIRAHATA*: The modern Japanese garden blended and fused Japanese and Western elements together. I think it was hard to create something like that.

●*TANI*: Usually, when you talk about the gardens of Kyoto, you think about the Temple gardens. I don't know if it was his intention or not but the fact that Ueji's gardens are completely free from any religious symbols is also unique.

●*SHIRAHATA*: The tradition of Kyoto gardens is in large part related to Buddhism. It's interesting to see that Ueji, who was the most famous gardener in Kyoto, did not create gardens containing religious symbols. But the fact that he created mostly gardens for the villas of businessmen and statesmen may have been a good opportunity for Ueji to design different gardens.

●*NAGATA*: Was it his intention to avoid religious symbols?

●*SHIRAHATA*: I don't think so. During the Meji period the economic power of the temples declined to the benefit of the businessmen so there was no more need for religious gardens.

●*NAGATA*: When exactly did Ueji become famous?

●*SHIRAHATA*: Ueji's reputation was enhanced after he created this garden in Murin-an with YAMAGATA Aritomo.

●*SASAOKA*: Has his name endured because it has been inherited over many generations?

●*TANI*: No, the gardens created by Ueji are not invariably maintained by his descendants.

●*NAGATA*: So Ueji's family does not always maintain the gardens he created. It means that as time passes, the owners change, the gardeners change… Even so, if today's people still say that this is an Ueji garden, it shows the great respect

ができる。建物の中にいながらにして、自然を身近に感じる。これは植治の庭についてのみ言えるのではなくて、日本建築の特性でもあります。縁を介して自然と建築とがやさしく繋がるのが日本の庭。

白幡●ただ、植治はなんにでも合わせられるというかね。（笑）あれだけ世俗に好かれた人はいないんじゃないかな。

永田●評価が揺るぎないものになってから、まだ日は浅いのですか。

白幡●いや、山縣有朋とともにこの無鄰庵をつくった時点で名声はグッと高まり、その評価が維持された。

笹岡●名が残るのは、植治の系譜が代々続いていることとも関わるのでしょうか。

谷●いや、植治の庭のすべてに当代の植治が関わっているわけではないですからね。たまたま碧雲荘には入っていますが。

永田●植治のつくった庭は代々の植治が引き継ぐ、責任をもちますということではないのですね。そうすると、最初の持ち主が満足していたお庭も、時代が変われば持ち主も変わり、手入れをする人も変わる……。それでも、「これは植治の庭だ」となるのは、みなさんが敬意をもって接しられるからでしょうね。

谷●とはいえ、真々庵は全面的に松下幸之助がつくり変えました。（笑）白い砂利を敷き詰めるなど、植治だとけっしてしなかったことをした。精神性を庭に盛り込もうとしたようですね。だから、あそこではいっさい食事などはせず、とにかく瞑想にふけったといいます。

だれが京都の庭園を継承するのか

白幡●植治の庭は基本的には元の形から変化していると思います。そのままを守れではなく、変更が許せる庭だからです。骨格はきっちりと残るようにしている。

笹岡●100年前そのままではないはずですね。逆に三玲は少しの変更も許さない。

白幡●植治だけが明治以降の日本の庭を引き受けていたわけではないが、彼の庭は残った。太い骨格があったからです。彼独自の水の流れ、水辺の石がそれです。木の扱いは控えめで、いろいろな樹種を受け入れる自然になっている。明治・大正期は、西洋のものを受け入れる熱気と流れがありましたが、それに迎合していただけでは日本の庭は潰れていたはずです。日本の表現、日本らしさをきちんと残したという点で、非凡な庭師だった。

谷●そうはいっても、維持にはものすごくお金がかかるんですよ。いま植治の庭の持ち主が次々と代わっていますね。ちょっとした庭でも個人では持ちきれない。

永田●個人の小さな庭でも春と秋に庭師さんに入ってもらおうとすると、半年間貯金しておかないととても払えない。（笑）でも、庭は手を入れるとぜんぜん違うんですものね。いつも感心するんです。

谷●碧雲荘は、なにかをちょっと修理するにも特殊な材料を使っていますからね。塗り一つがそうです。技術をもった左官さんも少なくなってきました。

しかも、このごろはペットが逃げ出したのか、アライグマが入り込んで池の鯉を食い散らすんですよ。ハクビシンとか猪もいます。花ショウブなどを養生していても、ぜんぶ掘り返される。庭師たちが懸命になって捕まえようとしますが、敵もさるものです。（笑）

they have for him.

Epilogue

●SHIRAHATA: I think that Ueji's gardens have changed with time. They have not been preserved as they were. But their basic structure was perfect, that is why they could be allowed to change.

●SASAOKA: They cannot be as they were 100 years ago for sure.

●SHIRAHATA: Ueji was not the only one to create gardens during the Meiji era but his gardens endure because of their perfect structure. Ueji's original streams and ponds are an example. His gardens integrate different elements. During the Meiji era there was a strong tendency to introduce western style. Ueji introduced western style but did not just copy it, using those new elements, he created the modern Japanese garden. In this sense, he was a revolutionary landscape gardener.

●TANI: However, the maintenance of those gardens is a heavy burden (laughs). This is why the owners sell them, even for a small garden, a private person cannot afford it.

●NAGATA: That's true, even in small gardens, gardeners have to come twice in a year, in spring and in autumn. If you do not save money for half a year, you cannot afford it (laughs). But gardens are much nicer after the gardeners come. I'm always very impressed by their skill.

●TANI: Also when you have to repair something, you need special materials and there are less and less artisans who are skilled in those traditional techniques so it costs a lot.

These days in the Hekiun-sō garden, there are raccoons that come and eat the carp. There are also wild boars that dig around the irises. They cause great damage to the garden. The gardeners are making an all-out effort to catch them but the animals are very clever too (laughs).

植治の生涯と仕事

西暦	年齢	出来事	作庭	所在地	関連する出来事
1860年	0歳	山城国乙訓郡西神足村（現・長岡京市）に山本藤五郎の二男として生まれる（4月5日）。幼名・源之助。			
1867年	7歳				山縣有朋、山口県萩市に無鄰庵を営む
1873年	13歳	神足小学校に通いはじめる。小学校制度ができた第1回卒業生となる			
1877年	17歳	小川治兵衛の四女・美津の婿養子として小川家に迎えられる（11月）			
1879年	19歳	1月、家督を受け継ぎ七代目小川治兵衛を襲名する			
1882年	22歳	長男保太郎（白楊）誕生			
1885年	25歳				琵琶湖疏水工事起工（1890年完成）
1886年	26歳				京都府は太政官布告第16号にもとづいて円山公園を公園地として指定（12月）
1887年	27歳				京都園芸業組合が組織される
1892年	32歳	鉄道合記共進会審査員を嘱託される			
1893年	33歳				平安神宮の造営に着手 円山公園の噴水に琵琶湖疏水から導水
1894年	34歳		並河靖之邸（現・並河靖之七宝記念館）庭園作庭 山縣有朋別荘「無鄰庵」庭園作庭着手（1896年了）	京都市東山区 京都市東山区	
1895年	35歳		平安神宮西神苑と中神苑の庭園工事着手（1916年了）	京都市左京区	第四回内国博覧会のために噴水用の導水管を延長、平安神宮に疏水が引かれる
1896年	36歳		帝国京都博物館（現・京都国立博物館）庭園作庭	京都市東山区茶屋町	山縣有朋は南禅寺の別荘新築にさいし、防火用として琵琶湖疏水の水を引く（8月2日）
1897年	37歳		賀陽宮須磨別邸庭園作庭 薩摩治兵衛別邸庭園作庭	神戸市須磨区 京都市左京区南禅寺	
1903年	43歳	清水吉次郎は別荘建築のため、川田龍吉から二条木屋町の土地を購入（8月）。小川治兵衛が代理人となる			京都市動物園開園。大正天皇（当時は皇太子）御成婚（1900年）を記念し寄付と市費で61種238点を飼育。疏水導水 無鄰庵洋館において日露開戦への方針を決める「無鄰庵会議」開かれる（4月21日）
1904年	44歳		京都府庁舎庭園作庭 都ホテル（現・ウェスティン都ホテル京都）の入口に滝築造（1985年に撤去）	京都市上京区 京都市東山区	日露戦争開戦（2月）。
1905年	45歳		市田弥一郎別荘「對龍山荘」庭園作庭 稲畑勝太郎邸「和楽庵」（現・何有荘）庭園作庭着手（1928年了）	京都市左京区 京都市左京区南禅寺	
1906年	46歳				不動産業の塚本与三次は「織宝苑」と「清流亭」の地に居を構え、南禅寺界隈の別荘地開発に取り組む 清水吉次郎、高台寺桝屋町（現・高台寺土井）を購入
1908年	48歳		清水吉次郎別荘「十牛庵」（現・高台寺土井）庭園作庭着手（1914年了）	京都市東山区桝屋町	
1909年	49歳		住友春翠別邸「慶沢園」庭園作庭着手（1910年了） 京都市商品陳列所庭園作庭着手（1910年了） 白楊、塚本与三次邸（現・織宝苑）庭園作庭着手（1913年了）	大阪市天王寺区 京都市左京区岡崎 京都市左京区	

西暦	年齢	出来事	作庭	所在地	関連する出来事
1910年	50歳		中井三郎兵衛邸「居然亭」庭園作庭 富山県庁貴賓室庭園設計	京都市左京区 富山市	
1911年	51歳	住友春翠とともに金沢兼六園を訪れる（10月）	「清風荘」庭園作庭着手（1913年了）	京都市左京区	第二疏水完成
1912年	52歳	京都御苑内改造工事、桂離宮・修学院離宮・二条離宮整備工事 「有芳園」の土地を入手			夷川発電所の建家完成 「對龍山荘」を訪れた黒田天外に植治が取材を受けた記事「新名園記（二）」所載の雑誌『日本　美術と工芸』第四号発行
1913年	53歳	黒田天外が白楊の案内で塚本与三次邸を訪れる（6月2日）	円山公園改良工事着手（1914年了） 京都伏見桃山御陵築造に携わる	京都市左京区 京都市伏見区	住友春翠、京都鹿ケ谷別邸敷地（現・有芳園の地）を植治より買収、造営に着手
1914年	54歳	大正天皇即位の大礼に伴い、儀式が行なわれる悠記・主基両殿の周囲に立てられる柴垣のほか周囲を作庭 京都大典記念博覧会審査員を嘱託される	住友春翠別邸（現・有芳園）庭園作庭着手（1920年了） 迎賓館庭園作庭	京都市左京区鹿ケ谷 所在地不明	
1915年	55歳	20年来の懇意である高橋箒庵と面談（6月19日）、高橋は「その資産100万円、古今無類の植木屋」と評す 京都府立植物園協議員を嘱託される	伏見桃山東陵築造に携わる	京都市伏見区	
1916年	56歳	高橋箒庵、植治の案内で稲畑邸（現・何有荘）と市田弥一郎邸（對龍山荘）を訪れる（11月19日）	光悦寺新席、露地作庭	京都市北区	
1917年	57歳	植治は高橋箒庵とともに大原三千院を訪れ、庭園補修案を相談（5月5日）	白楊、野村徳七の「碧雲荘」庭園作庭着手（1922年了）	京都市左京区	清水吉次郎、「十牛庵」（現・高台寺土井）を上西亀之助に売却
1918年	58歳		西園寺公望邸庭園作庭着手（1919年了） 村井吉兵衛邸庭園作庭着手（1919年了） 古河虎之助邸（現・旧古河庭園）庭園作庭着手（1919年了）	東京都千代田区駿河台 東京都港区 東京都北区西ヶ原	
1919年	59歳	住友春翠が慶沢園で先孝追悼の茶会を催す（11月）。植治も道具方を手伝う	住友春翠別邸庭園作庭 浜崎健吉別邸庭園作庭 山下亀三郎別邸庭園作庭 日下部久太郎邸庭園作庭 塚本忠治別邸庭園作庭 奥村猛別邸庭園作庭 山口県知事公舎庭園設計 西園寺公望別邸「坐漁荘」庭園作庭	京都市北区衣笠 京都市左京区南禅寺 神戸市中央区雲内 神戸市舞子町 岐阜県中津川市苗木町 京都市左京区鹿ケ谷 山口市 静岡市清水区興津	
1920年	60歳	京都博覧会審査員を嘱託される	阿部市太郎別邸庭園作庭 中井己二郎邸庭園作庭 津田藤五郎別邸庭園作庭 井村健次郎邸庭園作庭 下郷伝平別荘「春秋山荘」庭園作庭 仁清乾山茶寮庭園作庭 小津清左衛門別邸庭園作庭	京都市中京区二条木屋町 名古屋市白壁町 京都市東山区 京都市東山区八坂 京都市山科区 京都市東山区清水寺境内 京都市東山区五条	清水吉次郎、桝屋町の別荘を手放し、すぐ西の隣町に土地を購入（高台寺下河原町）、別荘の建設をはじめる
1921年	61歳		吉田卯之助別邸庭園作庭 鋳谷別邸庭園作庭 橋本儀兵衛邸庭園作庭 白楊、浅見又蔵別邸庭園作庭着手（未完）	京都市左京区南禅寺 山口県厚狭郡 京都市右京区嵯峨 京都市左京区聖護院	
1922年	62歳		大原孫三郎邸庭園改修着手（1927年了） 大原別邸の庭園作庭（1923年了） 小川睦之助邸庭園作庭	岡山県倉敷市 岡山県倉敷市 京都市左京区鹿ケ谷	山縣有朋85歳で没す（2月）
1923年	63歳		清水寺「南園」作庭	京都市東山区	

西暦	年齢	出来事	作庭	所在地	関連する出来事
1924年	64歳	京都園芸業組合の相談役に就任、1931年まで務める			
1925年	65歳		白楊、清浦奎吾別荘「喜寿庵」前庭作庭（現・佳水園） 住友吉左衛門本邸庭園設計	京都市東山区 神戸市	
1926年	66歳	白楊没す（12月28日）。45歳。聖護院の浅見又蔵別邸庭園、未完となる	薩摩治兵衛別邸庭園作庭 安宅弥吉邸庭園作庭 八坂神社神苑作庭着手（1927年了） 大倉恒吉邸庭園作庭着手（1927年了）	京都市左京区南禅寺 神戸市東灘区住吉 京都市東山区 京都市伏見区	「京都日出新聞」に「見識家の植治」掲載される（2月21日）
1927年	67歳	昭和大礼に伴い悠紀・主基両殿柴垣のほか周囲を作庭	松ヶ崎水源地苑園作庭 北垣国道邸庭園作庭着手（1928年了） 細川護立別邸「怡園」庭園作庭（1932年了） 光雲寺庭園作庭	京都市左京区松ヶ崎 京都市左京区松ヶ崎 京都市左京区 京都市左京区南禅寺	
1928年	68歳		清水吉次郎別荘第二次「十牛庵」庭園作庭 大原別邸（現・有隣荘）庭園作庭着手（1931年了） 岩倉具視旧邸跡庭園作庭 西園寺公望邸庭園作庭 岩崎小弥太邸庭園作庭着手（1930年了） 野村徳七別邸「碧雲荘」庭園第二期工事	京都市東山区高台寺下河原町 岡山県倉敷市 京都市左京区岩倉 東京都 東京都 京都市左京区	
1929年	69歳	昭和大礼跡復旧工事	島津源蔵邸庭園作庭 大宮庫吉邸庭園作庭 醍醐寺伝法院庭園作庭 奥村邸庭園作庭着手（1930年了） 西園寺公望別邸庭園作庭 松本邸庭園作庭庭園着手（1930年了）	京都市左京区二条木屋町 京都市伏見区 京都市伏見区 京都市東山区 静岡市清水区興津 京都市左京区南禅寺	
1930年	70歳		霊山築造着手（1931年了） 伴良太郎邸庭園作庭着手（1931年了）	京都市東山区 京都市東山区松原	
1931年	71歳		高山寺「遺香庵」露地作庭 東寺庭園作庭（現・小子房） 仁和寺庭園作庭 長尾欣弥邸庭園作庭 長尾欣弥別邸庭園作庭着手（1934年了） 生家・山本邸庭園作庭	京都市右京区 京都市南区 京都市右京区 東京都 神奈川県鎌倉市 京都府長岡京市	
1932年	72歳		大原別邸庭園作庭 護王神社庭園作庭 井上トモ邸庭園作庭 西村伊亮邸庭園作庭 長尾欣弥別邸庭園作庭着手（1934年了）	神戸市東灘区住吉 京都市上京区 京都市左京区 滋賀県 滋賀県大津市坂本	円山公園、国の名勝指定を受ける
1933年	73歳	植治没す（12月2日）。法名、寳樹院釈善光居士	岩崎小弥太邸（現・織宝苑）改造着手 住友旧邸庭園作庭 大徳寺庭園作庭 都ホテル「可楽庵露地」、「葵殿庭園」作庭着手（1934年了） 渡辺郁二別邸庭園作庭 小倉正恒邸庭園作庭着手（1934年了） 小川睦之助邸庭園作庭着手（1934年了）	京都市左京区 大阪市中央区鰻谷 京都市北区紫野 京都市東山区 京都市上京区 東京都 京都市東山区白川	

時代思潮と植治

白幡洋三郎　国際日本文化研究センター教授

　植治が独自の造園の境地を見出すきっかけとなる山縣有朋の別荘無鄰庵や平安神宮の庭園づくりにかかわった明治20年代の終わりごろ、つまり1890年代の日本はどのような社会状況にあったろうか。政治・社会面では日清戦争（1894-95）の混乱と活気があり、文化・芸術面では「古い」ものと「新しい」ものとが競っていた。「古い」のは芝居小屋で演じられる「歌舞伎」であり、決まった題材の「日本画」であり、座敷芸の「邦楽」である。他方「新しい」のは、シェークスピアの邦訳劇に代表される「西洋演劇」であり、生活を描く「洋画」であり、洋楽器が奏でる「西洋音楽」である。

　新しい文化・芸術思潮がわき起こるなかで、庭園の世界に植治は一見したところ新しい庭園様式を持ち込んではいない。少なくとも植治が示した様式や技法は従来の日本庭園の延長線上にあった。文化芸術分野の新しい風を庭園界に持ち込む試みがあってもかまわないはずなのに、なぜ植治は「新しい」西洋風、洋風庭園、洋式庭園を導入しなかったのだろうか。

　もちろん彼を支援したのは主に明治の新興富裕層・財界人であり、すなわち「新しい」社会勢力である。ところが彼らの多くが持った趣味のうち庭園とかかわるものは「古い」茶人趣味であった。庭園界のパトロンたちが好み、選んだのは西洋の様式ではなく日本の庭園様式であった。それは彼らの社会的な交際、社交に必要だったからである。

　植治の生涯最大のパトロンとされるのは、住友吉左衛門（春翠）である。大阪の住友家茶臼山本邸の慶沢園、京都の清風荘（西園寺公望の京都別邸）、鹿ケ谷の別邸・有芳園、衣笠別邸などの庭園を植治はつくった。これら吉左衛門のための造園で、植治はずいぶん江戸時代の大名庭園を意識し、また実際に大名庭園を模範にしたと思われる逸話が残っている。植治自身、「慶沢園は岡山後楽園を遥かに凌ぐ庭園になる」といった発言をしたり、造園の参考にするため吉左衛門のお供で金沢兼六園を見学に行ったりするなど、大名庭園は植治のアイデアの源泉であった。

　植治の造園は新しいクライアントが求める新しい欲求に応えるものであった。しかしそれは、過去と断絶したものではなく、むしろ過去の造園様式のなかで生み出された大名庭園の手法を生かして新しい用途に適応させた「新しさ」であったと私は思う。

The Spirit of the Meiji Era and Ueji

SHIRAHATA Yōzaburō
Professor, International Research Center for Japanese Studies

Let's take a look at the social background of Japan in the 1890's, during the period when Ueji was involved in landscaping the garden for Duke YAMAGATA Aritomo's villa Murin-an and that of the Heian-jingū shrine, works that made him seize the opportunity to open up his own unique territory in landscape design. In those days, the chaos and vigor that originated from the Japan-Chinese War (1894-95) formed the political and social background, causing contests to arise between the "new" and the "old" in the country's cultural and artistic arenas.

Examples of things that were considered "old" are: "Kabuki" performed in traditional theaters, "Japanese paintings" that only employ traditional materials and "Japanese music" which was salon music performed mainly by geishas. On the other hand, "Western theater dramas" such as Japanese translations of Shakespearean plays, "Western paintings" that portrayed everyday life and "Western music" performed with Western instruments are examples of things that were considered "new."

Glancing at his work, in spite of the rise of new cultural and artistic currents of thought, Ueji seems to have been unenthusiastic about bringing new landscaping styles into his work. At least, those styles and techniques Ueji came up with were an extention of traditional Japanese gardening. Ueji must have had the chance to adopt new cultural and artistic trends in his work, but the fact is that he did not introduce the "new" western style garden to his work nor make gardens with a western feel.

The group that supported Ueji was composed of individuals of the new wealthy class and business leaders of the Meiji era, in other words, the

清風荘は、住友家が所有し、縁戚関係にあり内閣総理大臣も務めた西園寺公望の京都別邸として提供された。現在は京都大学に寄贈・管理されている〈撮影・編集部〉

Seifū-sō garden in Kyoto. Used by the Duke SAIONJI Kinmochi who was a relative of the owner, the SUMITOMO family. It is currently being managed by Kyoto University to which it was donated (photograph by the editorial staff)

大名庭園としての風格を
そなえた對龍山荘

Tairyū-Sansō garden was garbed with the distinctive style of a daimyo's garden

"new" social forces. However, among their many cultural interests, their taste for things related to gardening was similar to that of "old" tea masters. Therefore, many of the patrons of the gardening world naturally chose the Japanese rather than Western style for their gardens.

Ueji's greatest patron is said to have been SUMITOMO Kichizaemon. Therefore, Ueji was involved in landscaping many famous gardens on the SUMITOMOS' estates including: the Keitaku-en garden at their principal residence in Osaka, the Seifū-sō garden (used as Duke SAIONJI Kinmochi's villa), the Yuhō-en garden and other villas in Kyoto. When gardening for SUMITOMO, Ueji was very conscious of following the style of daimyos' garden (feudal lords' gardens) established during the Edo era. In fact, there is an anecdote suggesting that Ueji might actually have modeled these gardens after the classic daimyos' gardens. Ueji commented that "In the end, SUMITOMO's Keitaku-en garden will excel the Koraku-en daimyo's garden in Okayama." He also traveled to Kanazawa as SUMITOMO's attendant to draw inspiration from the landscaping of the Kenroku-en daimyo's garden; daimyos' gardens were indeed the source of Ueji's ideas.

Though Ueji's landscaping met the new demands of clients whose social class had risen recently, it was not something that was broken off from the tradition of the past. It was an approach that had its roots in daimyos' gardens, a style that arose from traditional Japanese landscape design. In my view, Ueji's landscaping was "new" in the way he adapted the traditional daimyo's garden style to new purposes and needs of the Meiji era.

庭園用語の解説

小野健吉著『日本庭園事典』、京都林泉協会編『日本庭園鑑賞便覧』を参考に編集部で作成しました。

素材

◎青石　　　　　　　　　あおいし
青緑色を帯びた庭石の総称。結晶片岩をさすことが多い。埼玉県の三波石、和歌山県紀ノ川の紀州青石、四国で産出する阿波青石と伊予青石など。石組、石橋、景石などに用いる。

◎貴船石　　　　　　　　きぶねいし
京都市の加茂川上流の貴船地区で産する輝緑凝灰岩、水成岩などの総称。貴船糸石、貴船紫、貴船蓬、虎石、貴船真黒などの名が与えられ、珍重される。景石、沓脱石、手水鉢、飛び石などに用いるが、現在はほとんど採取できない。

◎鞍馬石　　　　　　　　くらまいし
京都鞍馬山周辺でとれる閃緑岩。石に含まれる鉄分によって表面は茶褐色。類似の石では、丹波鞍馬石や岡山万成石、甲州鞍馬石が知られる。植治は沓脱石として用いたほか、小ぶりの鞍馬石を川床の底石として用いて、その色目を楽しめるよう工夫した。

◎チャート　　　　　　　chert
珪質の堆積岩で、きめこまかで固い。獣角状の光沢があり、赤褐色または薄黒いものが多い。放散虫の遺骸が深海底などに堆積し固結してできた放散虫チャートは、層状が普通。かつては角岩とも呼ばれた。

◎守山石　　　　　　　　もりやまいし
褶曲した縞目が特徴の水成岩。滋賀県の琵琶湖西岸の志賀町守山に産出する。江州チャリ石ともいう。平安神宮東神苑築造の際などに、植治は疏水の舟運を利用して大量に京都に持ち込んだ。

組み石

◎石組　　　　　　　　　いしぐみ
「いわぐみ」と呼ぶこともあり、「岩組」の字をあてることもある。石を組み合わせて配置することをいう。その位置、役割により、滝石組、三尊石組などの名称が与えられる。水を用いないで庭景をつくる枯山水では、中心的な構成要素となることが多い。

◎岩島　　　　　　　　　いわしま
池庭に配した石の島。水面上に1石が姿を見せる場合と、組み合った複数の石が姿をあらわす場合とがある。

◎沢飛石　　　　　　　　さわとびいし
池や流れを人が渡るために配置した石。加工石も利用する。実用のためだけでなく、景としても用いる。沢飛びとも、沢渡りともいう。

◎敷石　　　　　　　　　しきいし
とくに雨の日の人の歩行を助ける石材舗装。加工石を敷く切石敷石、加工しない玉石を敷く玉石敷、加工石と自然石とを交える寄石敷などの種類がある。園路だけでなく、広場的な舗装の場合にもいうが、畳石・延段は敷石の園路をいう。

◎州浜　　　　　　　　　すはま
曲線を伴った広い砂浜を庭園内に意匠化したもの。ゆるやかな勾配をつけて小石を敷き詰めて池の護岸にも、枯山水にも用いられる。奈良時代から確立した手法とみられる。

◎瀬落ち　　　　　　　　せおち
浅瀬に大きめの石を用いて流れに段差をつけ、せせらぎの音をつくる効果と、川の流れ・景の変化を目的とした手法。植治が得意とした。

◎滝　　　　　　　　　　たき
本来は急傾斜の斜面を勢いよく流下する水の流れを指す。古代から、庭の重要な構成要素としてつくられる。石の表面を流れる「伝い落ち」の滝、糸のように水が落ちる「糸落ち」の滝などの手法がある。

◎飛び石　　　　　　　　とびいし
露地や庭園内を、人が伝い歩くために配置した石。庭園に用いられるようになったのは、露地の成立した安土桃山時代から。上面の平らな自然石を用いることが多いが、加工石などの加工石を用いることもある。直打ち、二三連、三四連、千鳥打ちなどがある。

配石

◎景石　　　　　　　　　けいせき
景観をつくるための庭石。1石だけの場合と、数石で組む場合とがある。

◎捨石　　　　　　　　　すていし
山間にさりげなくある石のように一見無造作に石を据える手法のこと。普通は1石で、比較的大ぶりであることが多い。江戸末期から明治期にかけて確立された手法で、植治の得意の空間の生かし方。露地の飛び石の近くに据えて、飛び石の景色を整える小さな石を指すこともある。

◎立石　　　　　　　　　たていし
1200年前後に書かれた造園の秘伝書『作庭記』では、石を据えることを「石を立てる」と表現している。現在では、じっさいに石を立てる場合のみを指す。滝の石組、護岸、岩島などに多く用いられる。立石に対し、地に伏すように据える庭石は伏石という。

◎伏石　　　　　　　　　ふせいし
地面に伏せた形で据えられた石。空間の釣りあいをとるアクセントをつくる。

役石

◎役石　　　　　　　　　やくいし
作庭上の約束事にしたがって据えられる石のこと。江戸中期以降に生まれた用語と考えられている。滝の水落石・滝添石・滝挟石・脇石・中石・水分石、遣り水の廻石・横石・水越の石・端挟石、露地の貴人石・連客石・客石・鐘聞石・乗越石・亭主石、蹲踞の手燭石・湯桶石・前石、飛び石の踏分石・額見石、茶室の軒内の刀掛石など、役割ごとに多くの種類と名称がある。

◎伽藍石　　　　　　　　がらんいし
廃寺・廃社の建物の礎石。おもに飛び石として用いられる。明治から大正期にとくに流行し、自然石を新たに加工して用いることが多くなった。

◎沓脱石　　　　　　　　くつぬぎいし
玄関や、庭に面した縁側・濡縁に接して置く石。履物の着脱に便利なように、やや細長く表面の平らな石を用いる。加工石だけでなく自然石も使用する。

◎手水鉢　　　　　　　　ちょうずばち
茶庭に、客が手を洗い、口をすすぐために設けられた水鉢。庭園に持ち込まれるようになったのは、露地の形式が整ってきた千利休のころと見られる。露地の蹲踞の中心をなす蹲踞手水鉢と、建物の縁先に置かれる縁先手水鉢の二つのタイプがある。自然石や加工石に水穴を穿って用いる。

◎橋添石　　　　　　　　はしぞえいし
橋の両端両側に1石ずつ4個置くのが基本だが、1石または2石を省略することも多い。石の高さをそれぞれ違えることで変化をつけることが一般的。橋挟石とも、袂石ともいい、平安時代から用いられてきた手法。

◎根石　　　　　　　　　ねいし
礎石。建物などの柱を支える石のこと。池に建物を張りださせた植治の庭では重要な役割を果たす。

水と流れ

◎流れ　　　　　　　　　ながれ
庭園の小川の総称。平安・鎌倉期の寝殿造庭園の流れは遣り水とよばれる。池への導水路または池からの排水路の機能をもつ。日本の庭園史のきわめて早い段階に出現している。

◎遣り水　　　　　　　　やりみず
庭園内に設けられた蛇行する流路。幅は狭く浅いもので、池に導水する目的もある。『作庭記』には、水を流す方向にも言及しているのは、陰陽五行説などにもとづくからである。さらに、石は護岸の全面に置くのではなく、水があたって折り返す場所には廻り石を置くなど合理的な配置を勧めている。底

石、水切りの石、詰石、水越の石など、機能ごとに名前が与えられている。

思想・信仰

◎陰陽五行説　いんようごぎょうせつ
古代中国にはじまる思想。陰陽論と五行説とで構成される。陰陽論では、日・火・夏・南・男などの陽と、月・水・冬・北・女などの陰との相互作用によって万物が創造されるとする。五行説では、万物を構成する木・火・土・金・水の五元素の相互作用ですべての物事・人事が進行するとを説く。『作庭記』から江戸期の造園の秘伝書に至るまで、この思想にもとづく記述を見ることができる。

◎陰陽石　いんようせき
男女の生殖器をあらわす一組みの石。立石は男性を象徴する陽石、伏石などは女性を象徴する陰石として、陰陽和合・子孫繁栄を表現する。江戸時代の大名庭園などに見られる。

◎神仙蓬莱　しんせんほうらい
古代の日本に伝わった古い中国の思想。不老不死の仙人が住む理想郷として考えられ、道教思想に取り込まれて広まり庭園でも古くから人が思う理想の山や海島に見立て、池を海の表現とし、その中心を神仙蓬莱島などとして崇めた。地主の永寿を祈るものであり、鶴島も亀島も含まれる。日本庭園を構成する基礎の一つになった。

形式・様式

◎池庭　いけにわ
池のある庭のこと。日本庭園は、様式的には池庭・枯山水・露地の三つに大きく分類できる。なかでも池庭はもっとも古くからある形式である。池泉、林泉、園池、泉石、泉水、泉閣、苑林とも書く。湧き水を水源とするほか、かつての河床伏流水や潮の干満を利用する場合もある。植治は琵琶湖疏水を利用して京都東山近辺の数多くの別荘に大規模の池庭をつくった。

◎廻遊式　かいゆうしき
庭内を歩きながら観賞あるいは宴遊する庭の形式のこと。江戸初期の池庭に多く、その場合は池泉廻遊式という。

広い敷地に大きな池を中心として築山や平場をしつらえ、御殿や茶室などの建物を随所に配す構成。

◎枯山水　かれさんすい
『作庭記』にも枯山水の文字を見るが、平安期から室町初期にかけては池庭や遣り水のほとりに石組だけで山水を表現した庭という概念であった。現在では、水を用いずに石や白砂などで水やその流れを表現した庭（枯滝、枯流れ、枯池）をさす。夢窓疎石の西芳寺にはじまる。龍安寺の庭がよく知られる。

◎寝殿造庭園　しんでんづくりていえん
平安時代の貴族や皇族の寝殿造りの住居に設置した庭園の様式。典型的な庭園は、寝殿と東西の対屋、それを結ぶ渡殿、対屋から南に伸びる中門廊などで囲まれた空間につくられた。寝殿前の大きな広場の南には池と中島を穿ち、橋を据えた。水は北東から流れくる遣り水で運ぶという姿だった。

◎茶庭　ちゃにわ
「ちゃてい」ともいう。茶室にともなう庭園。露地と同じ意味で用いられることが多いが、茶室と書院にともなう庭という広い意味がある。

◎中島　なかじま
池庭に設けられる島。半島を示す出島と明確に区別するための用語。園池の中央に位置するとはかぎらない。

◎野筋　のすじ
帯状のゆるやかな起伏をつくることで野の風景を表現する技法とその地形。池や遣り水と関わることが多い。

◎露地　ろじ
露地門から茶室に至るまでの茶庭のこと。室町末期から茶室とともにつくられた。露地、路地、路次、廬地、炉地などとも書く。花木は避けてカシ類などの常緑樹を植える。日本庭園の様式に大きな影響を及ぼした。中門を境とした外露地と内露地という区切りのある二重露地の茶庭もある。内露地は茶室のある区画をいう。内露地には内腰掛、蹲踞、井戸などを設ける。

技法・効果

◎糸落ち　いとおち
滝の水を落とす手法の一つで、落水をいくつもの筋に分け、糸のように筋を引かせる。滝落の石の端に凹凸がたくさんある石を水落石として使用することで糸を引く。その水落石をわずかに仰向かせ、石の表面にそって水を伝い落とす手法を「伝い落ち」とよぶ。

◎刈込　かりこみ
生垣や庭木を剪定して形を整えたもの。ツツジやサツキなど常緑の小樹が多い。枯山水では刈込で遠山などを象徴的に表現する。大刈込、小刈込、丸、波など、形によって異なる呼称がある。

◎借景　しゃっけい
庭園の外の自然や風物を背景、または点景として庭園に取り入れること。江戸時代の庭園では借景の手法が盛んに用いられた。京都では、比叡山を借景にした円通寺と正伝寺が名高い。明治期もよく利用され、植治は無鄰菴や對龍山荘などの庭で東山を巧みに取り入れている。

◎蛇籠　じゃかご
丸く細長く粗く編んだ籠の中に、栗石や砕石などを詰めたもの。河川工事の護岸・水制などに用いる。竹蛇籠、粗朶籠、鉄線蛇籠などがある。石籠、じゃことも いう。

◎地割　じわり
庭の基本設計というべきもので、池の形や島の配置、築山の設け方、主要石の配置、橋の架け方など、おおよその平面計画のこと。

◎築山　つきやま
庭園内に土で築いた山。池と組み合わせて庭園の重要な構成要素となる。枯山水でも山を表現する小規模の築山を築く事例もある。江戸期の廻遊式庭園などには大規模な築山が築かれるようになったのは、そこに登って眺望を楽しむ目的もあった。

◎見立て　みたて
京都をはじめとする日本文化の特徴の

一つ。本来とは別のものを使って、それらしく見せたり、なぞらえたりする手法。象徴的であったり、示唆的であったりと、見る人の感性や知性に訴える。和歌・俳諧・戯作文学・歌舞伎などの芸術表現の一技法としても用いられる。庭では、州浜、鶴亀石、蓬莱山、三尊石などがその典型。

石造物

◎石燈籠　いしどうろう
点灯設備のある石造品。仏教伝来とともに中国から伝えられ、神仏に灯明をあげるために使用された。基礎、竿、中台、火袋笠、宝珠で構成される。これらが茶庭に利用されることで種々の形式が生まれ、庭中にも置かれるようになった。

◎蹲踞　つくばい
茶室近くの露地に設けられる手水のための施設。蹲踞（そんきょ）の姿勢で手水を使うところからきている。手水鉢の手前の前石、左右の手燭（てしょく）石と湯桶石などの役石で構成される。流れの中に手水鉢を据える流れ蹲踞、周辺の地面から一段下がったところに据える降り蹲踞などもある。

建築・建造物

◎書院　しょいん
狭義には、縁側に張りだした造りつけの机のこと。前面には明かりをとる障子が設けられる。そのうえで、床の間や違い棚などをそなえ、儀式や客の接待に使われる部屋のこともさす。書院を中心に構成する書院造りの建物全体をさすこともある。

◎数寄屋造り　すきやづくり
茶室の初期の呼称。茶室建築の技法を取り入れた住宅を数寄屋・数寄屋建築と称す。数奇とも書く。

◎茶室　ちゃしつ
安土桃山時代に成立した茶会用の部屋。書院の座敷に準じた書院茶室と、質素な田舎を模した草庵風茶室とがある。

◎築地塀　ついじべい
土塀の上に屋根を葺いた形式。古くは、土を盛り上げて固めただけであった。

掲載庭園の所在地と交通案内

社寺名など	所在地	郵便番号	電話	交通案内	その他
並河靖之七宝記念館	京都市東山区三条通北裏 白川筋東入る堀池町388	605-0038	075-752-3277	■地下鉄東西線「東山駅」下車1番出口より徒歩3分 ■市バス201、202、203、206系統「東山三条」下車徒歩5分	有料
無鄰菴	京都市左京区南禅寺草川町31	606-8437	075-771-3909	■地下鉄東西線「蹴上駅」下車、徒歩約7分 ■市バス5系統「神宮道」下車、徒歩10分	有料
平安神宮	京都市左京区岡崎西天王町97	606-8341	075-761-0221	■地下鉄東西線「東山駅」下車、徒歩10分 ■市バス5系統「京都会館・美術館前」下車すぐ	有料
何有荘	京都市左京区南禅寺福地町46	606-8435			非公開
円山公園	京都市東山区円山町473	605-0001	075-561-0533	■京阪四条駅下車、徒歩10分 ■市バス201、202、203、206「祇園」下車、徒歩5分	無料
碧雲荘	京都市左京区南禅寺下河原町37	606-8434			特別公開のみ
高台寺土井	京都市東山区高台寺桝屋町353	605-0826	075-561-0309	■市バス206系統「清水道」下車、徒歩6分 ■市バス207系統「東山安井」下車、徒歩6分	利用客のみ
ウェスティン 都ホテル京都	京都市東山区粟田口華頂町1	605-0052	075-771-7111	■地下鉄東西線「蹴上駅」下車すぐ	予約制

Site	Location	Postal Code	Telephone	Access	Entrance Fees
Namikawa Cloisonné Museum of Kyoto	388 Horiike-cho Higashiyama-ku Kyoto-shi	605-0038	075-752-3277	* 3 min. walk from the subway Tozai line Higashiyama Stasion * 5 min. walk from the Higashiyama Sanjo bus stop (100, 201, 202, 203, 206)	Entrance Fees
Murin-an	31 Kusakawa-cho Nanzen-ji Sakyo-ku Kyoto-shi	606-8437	075-771-3909	* 7min. walk from the subway Tozai line Keage Station * 10 min. walk from the Jingu-michi bus stop	Entrance Fees
Heian-jingū	97 Nishitenno-cho Okazaki Sakyo-ku Kyoto-shi	606-8341	075-761-0221	* 10 min. walk from the subway Tozai line Higashiyama Station * Right next to the Kyoto Kaikan Bijyutsukan-mae bus stop	Entrance Fees
Kaiu-sō	46 Fukuchi-cho Nanzen-ji Sakyo-ku Kyoto-shi				Private
Maruyama Park	473 Maruyama-cho Higashiyama-ku Kyoto-shi	605-0001	075-561-0533	* 10 min. walk from the Keihan line Shijo Station * 5 min. walk from the Gion bus stop (100, 201, 202, 203, 206)	Entrance Free
Hekiun-sō	37-2 Shimogawara-cho Nanzen-ji Kyoto-shi				Private
Kōdaiji-Doi	353 Masuya-cho Kodai-ji Higashiyama-ku Kyoto-shi	605-0826	075-561-0309	* 6min. walk from the Kiyomizu-michi bus stop (100, 201, 202, 203, 206, 207)	Clients Only
Westin Miyako Kyoto	1 Awataguchikacho-cho Higashiyama-ku Kyoto-shi	605-0052	075-771-7111	* Right next to from the subway Tozai line Keage Station	Clients Only

見学時のマナー

心地よい見学をすごすには、一人ひとりの心がけが大切です。
1. 室内では、襖や障子などを傷をつけないよう、リュックサックなどは手に持ってください。
2. 建具などから50センチ以上離れて見学してください。
3. 聖なる空間・儀式空間には、入らないでください。
4. 装飾品や家具には、手を触れないでください。
5. 畳の部屋には、清潔な靴下で、ズボンの裾を上げてお入りください。
6. 庭では飛び石伝いに歩き、石に触れたり、白砂や苔などを踏んだりしないでください。
7. 写真撮影は、当該施設の規則・指導にしたがってください。
8. 飲食、タバコはご遠慮ください。大声で騒いだり走り廻ったりも自制してください。

Manners for visiting Japanese Gardens

Please respect these manners so that everybody can enjoy the space.
1. When you are inside, take off your bag and take care of the sliding doors.
2. Please stay away from the sliding doors and other fittings.
3. Do not stand in sacred or ceremonial spaces.
4. Do not touch the sacred sculptures or other decorations.
5. Wear clean socks and ensure your trouser cuffs are not dragging when you walk on the tatami (straw mats).
6. While walking in the garden, please follow the stepping stones and refrain from walking in the gravel or on the moss.
7. Please obey the rules regarding pictures and videos in each garden.
8. Don't eat, drink or smoke. Refrain from speaking loudly and running around.

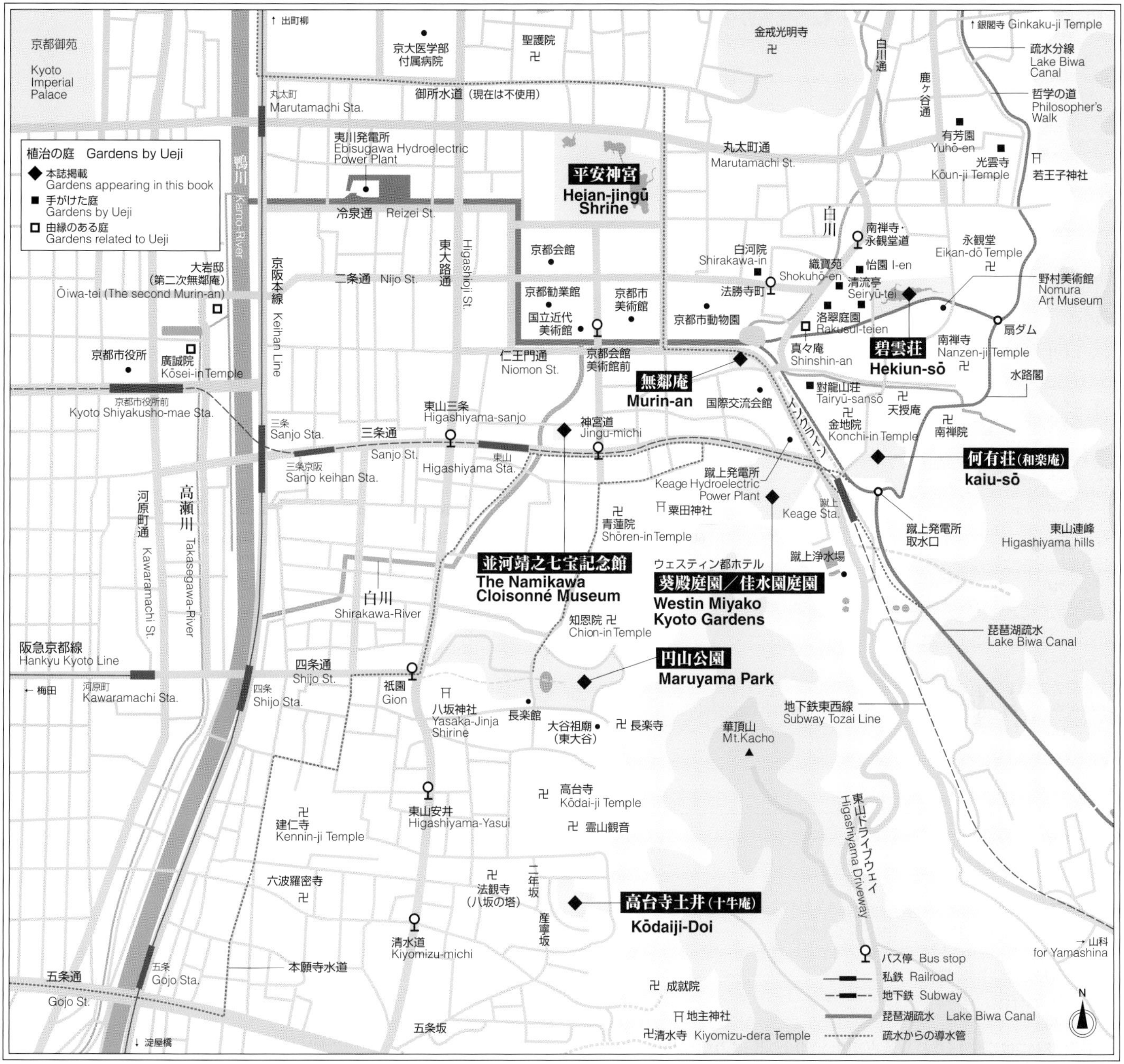

植治の庭　Gardens by Ueji
本誌掲載
Gardens appearing in this book
手がけた庭
Gardens by Ueji
由縁のある庭
Gardens related to Ueji
京都御苑
Kyoto Imperial Palace
↑ 出町柳
京大医学部付属病院
聖護院
金戒光明寺
白川通
↑ 銀閣寺 Ginkaku-ji Temple
疏水分線
Lake Biwa Canal
哲学の道
Philosopher's Walk
鹿ケ谷通
丸太町
Marutamachi Sta.
御所水道（現在は不使用）
夷川発電所
Ebisugawa Hydroelectric Power Plant
丸太町通
Marutamachi St.
有芳園
Yuhō-en
光雲寺
Kōun-ji Temple
若王子神社
平安神宮
Heian-jingū Shrine
鴨川
Kamo-River
冷泉通　Reizei St.
白川
南禅寺・永観堂道
永観堂
Eikan-dō Temple
京都会館
白河院
Shirakawa-in
織寶苑
Shokuhō-en
怡園 I-en
清流亭
Seiryū-tei
野村美術館
Nomura Art Museum
大岩邸
（第二次無鄰庵）
Ōiwa-tei (The second Murin-an)
京阪本線
Keihan Line
二条通　Nijo St.
東大路通
Higashioji St.
京都勧業館
京都市美術館
法勝寺町
京都市動物園
洛翠庭園
Rakusui-teien
国立近代美術館
扇ダム
真々庵
Shinshin-an
碧雲荘
Hekiun-sō
南禅寺
Nanzen-ji Temple
京都市役所
廣誠院
Kōsei-in Temple
仁王門通
Niomon St.
京都会館美術館前
無鄰庵
Murin-an
水路閣
京都市役所前
Kyoto Shiyakusho-mae Sta.
國際交流会館
對龍山荘
Tairyū-sansō
天授庵
東山三条
Higashiyama-sanjo
神宮道
Jingu-michi
インクライン
金地院
Konchi-in Temple
南禅院
三条
Sanjo Sta.
三条通
Sanjo St.
東山
Higashiyama Sta.
三条京阪
Sanjo keihan Sta.
何有荘（和楽庵）
kaiu-sō
蹴上発電所
Keage Hydroelectric Power Plant
粟田神社
蹴上
Keage Sta.
蹴上発電所取水口
東山連峰
Higashiyama hills
河原町通
Kawaramachi St.
高瀬川
Takasegawa-River
青蓮院
Shōren-in Temple
蹴上浄水場
並河靖之七宝記念館
The Namikawa Cloisonné Museum
ウェスティン都ホテル
葵殿庭園／佳水園庭園
Westin Miyako Kyoto Gardens
白川
Shirakawa-River
知恩院
Chion-in Temple
琵琶湖疏水
Lake Biwa Canal
阪急京都線
Hankyu Kyoto Line
四条通
Shijo St.
円山公園
Maruyama Park
← 梅田
河原町
Kawaramachi Sta.
四条
Shijo Sta.
祇園
Gion
八坂神社
Yasaka-Jinja Shirine
長楽館
大谷祖廟（東大谷）
長楽寺
華頂山
Mt.Kacho
地下鉄東西線
Subway Tozai Line
東山安井
Higashiyama-Yasui
高台寺
Kōdai-ji Temple
霊山観音
建仁寺
Kennin-ji Temple
東山ドライブウェイ
Higashiyama Driveway
六波羅密寺
法観寺（八坂の塔）
二年坂
産寧坂
高台寺土井（十牛庵）
Kōdaiji-Doi
清水道
Kiyomizu-michi
本願寺水道
五条
Gojo Sta.
五条通
Gojo St.
→ 山科
for Yamashina
バス停 Bus stop
私鉄 Railroad
地下鉄 Subway
琵琶湖疏水　Lake Biwa Canal
疏水からの導水管
成就院
地主神社
清水寺 Kiyomizu-dera Temple
五条坂
↓ 淀屋橋
N

◇協力いただいた団体など
（五十音順・敬称略）
稲畑産業株式会社
ウェスティン都ホテル京都
株式会社津多家
京都市文化市民局文化芸術企画課
京都市建設局緑地管理課
財団法人 並河靖之七宝記念館
財団法人 野村文華財団 野村美術館
財団法人 山縣有朋記念館
平安神宮
碧雲荘
料亭・高台寺土井

◇協力いただいた方がた
（五十音順・敬称略）
尼﨑博正
小野健吉
加藤友規
笹岡隆甫
佐藤昭夫
佐野藤右衛門
白幡洋三郎
谷 晃
永田 萌
日向 進
森本幸裕
矢ヶ崎善太郎

◇参考文献：
黒田天外『名家歴訪録（上編）』黒田譲、1899
黒田天外『江湖快心録』山田直三郎、1901
黒田天外『續江湖快心録』山田聖華書房、1907
黒田天外『續々江湖快心録』山田芸艸堂、1913
山根徳太郎編『小川治兵衛』小川金三、1965
京都大学造園学研究室編『造園の歴史と文化』養賢堂、1987
尼﨑博正編、田畑みなお撮影『植治の庭——小川治兵衛の世界』淡交社、1990
尼﨑博正著、田畑みなお撮影『石と水の意匠——植治の造園技法』淡交社、1992
白幡洋三郎『大名庭園——江戸の饗宴』講談社、1997
11代小川治兵衞監修『「植治の庭」を歩いてみませんか
　　　　　　　　　　——洛翠庭園・無鄰菴庭園』白川書院、2004
小野健吉『日本庭園事典』岩波書店、2004
加藤哲弘、中川理、並木誠士編『東山／京都風景論』昭和堂、2006
尼﨑博正監修、田畑みなお撮影『對龍山荘——植治と島藤の技』淡交社、2007

シリーズ 京の庭の巨匠たち2
植治 七代目小川治兵衞——手を加えた自然にこそ自然がある

2008年3月20日発行

写　真	田畑みなお
監　修	白幡洋三郎
発行所	京都通信社 京都市中京区室町通御池上る御池之町309　〒604-0022 電話 075-211-2340　http://www.kyoto-info.com/kyoto/
発行人	中村基衞
編　集	中村基衞＋マレス・エマニュエル
翻　訳	引原忠夫、ラッセル・トロット、キャサリン・パワサラト、加藤博之祐
装　丁	納富進＋秋葉敦子
製　版	豊和写真製版株式会社
印　刷	サンテック印刷株式会社
製　本	株式会社吉田三誠堂製本所

©2008 京都通信社
Printed in Japan　ISBN978-4-903473-02-4

The Great Masters of Gardens of Kyoto 2
UEJI, The Genius of Water and Stone

Photographs by:
TABATA Minao

Supervision by:
SHIRAHATA Yōzaburō

Published by:
Kyoto Tsushinsha Press
309 Oike-no-cho Nakagyo-ku Kyoto 604-0022
http://www.kyoto-info.com/kyoto/

Editor:
Emmanuel MARES

Translated by:
HIKIHARA Tadao, Russell TROTT, Catherine PAWASARAT, KATŌ Hironosuke

Designed by:
NŌTOMI Susumu, AKIBA Atsuko

First published:
March 2008